D0409010

Fool's Gold

OTHER BOOKS BY ROB SCHULTHEIS

Bone Games

The Hidden West

Night Letters

Fool's Gold

Lives, Loves, and Misadventures
in the Four Corners Country

Rob Schultheis

THE LYONS PRESS

Copyright © 2000 by Rob Schultheis
All rights reserved. No part of this book may be reproduced in any manner
without the express written consent of the publisher, except in the case of
brief excerpts in critical reviews and articles.
All inquiries should be addressed to:
The Lyons Press, 123 West 18 Street, New York, NY 10011

Printed in the United States of America

1 3 5 7 9 10 8 6 4 2

Some of these essays have previously appeared in the *Washington Post*, the
Telluride Daily Planet, *Telluride* magazine, and *Inside/Outside*.

Library of Congress Cataloging-in-Publication Data is available on file.

For Alexandra Schultheis

To the Old-Timers—George and Gay Cappis,
Joe Vigil, Whispering Jim and Shamrock Dalpez;
Senior Mahoney, Irene Visintin, and Elvira Wunderlich;
the Goldsworthys; "Fast Jack" and Daveen Pera.

Contents

Going Up the Country   1

The Lay of the Land   15

The Goldsworthy Shack   23

Hardrock Days   27

The Sweetest Time   35

Law and Order, San Juan–Style   43

Disappointment Valley   51

The Black Book   57

Cabin Fever   61

Mountain Women   71

Killers of the Dream   87

Ghost Stories   97

San Juan Miracles   105

Summertime   109

Rock of Ages   119

The Great American Underground   129

I Know It's Only Rock & Roll, but Nizhoni'!   137

Sacred Waters   145

The Last Jew in Oiltown   161

Tall Tales   167

Running the Rockies   177

Contents

Dancing in Circular Time   *181*
Tenderfoot Blues   *185*
Flammulated Owl   *191*
Beaver Pond   *197*
Winter's Tale   *209*
The Blue Light   *217*
Home Sweet Mountain Home   *231*

Going Up the Country

I first moved down into the San Juan Mountains, near where Colorado, Utah, New Mexico, and Arizona come together, back in 1973. Telluride, Colorado—8,750 feet and change above sea level, high in a dead-end chasm in the mountains. Deep, deep in the gnarly heart of the Rockies.

Moving "up the country," in the words of the sixties Canned Heat song, has been a popular American countercultural option for centuries. In 1625 one of the very first New England colonists, Thomas Morton, fled from Plymouth Colony into the wilderness and built his own pagan settlement, in cooperation with the local Indians, called Merry-Mount. (Outraged by Morton's drinking and partying, his pagan poetry-reciting, and not least his tolerance and love for the local "savages," the Pilgrims

1

burned Merry-Mount down and shipped Morton back to England in chains.)

Then there's Thoreau, of course, and the fur-trapping Mountain Men, and later the Beats; and the hippie communards, with their tepees, adobes, rammed-earth pithouses, and geodesic domes. I was a belated part of an American tradition that said, "Turn your back on the cities, the hassles, the crowds, the artificial realm of fame and fortune, politics and history. Head for the hills."

It wasn't surprising, really, given my life up to that point. I had grown up in a diplomatic (read C.I.A.) family that roamed nomadically through the Far East during my childhood. This was the era of the hot-enough-to-hurt Cold War with China, and my father, fluent in several dialects of Chinese and a veteran of the 14th Air Force in Chungking during World War II, was one of those frontline tricksters whose job it was to embarrass, obstruct, and isolate the malign Marxist behemoth. We accompanied him from Hong Kong to the Philippines to Japan as he carried on his wacky campaign: smuggling a ninety-year-old high lama, a living Buddha, out of Inner Mongolia one step ahead of the atheist truth squads; parachuting young Chinese into the hinterlands of Yunnan and Sinkiang to raise hell; arranging to purloin a suitcase full of Chinese money bound for Africa to highjack an election.

I remember one cocktail party, at our house high on Victoria Peak overlooking Hong Kong Harbor, at which my dad and his shadowy guests sluiced down manhattans and dry martinis while they uncrated a shipment of Browning automatic rifles and .50-

caliber machine guns carefully sanitized as to place of origin. There was a framed photo on the living room wall of my father and my mother, who was born in China and could chatter away in Mandarin like a native, dining with the Tong Boss of Macao and his Number One Wife; the Boss, a mild-looking middle-aged Fukienese, was hiring out his hatchet men to counter-whack assassins sent from the People's Republic to kill Enemies of the State. Among these Enemies was my father: after the PRC managed to get a hit man into our villa one night—Dad slept with a .45 under his pillow, and got off a shot at the man, who fled—my brother and I got our own bodyguard, a big friendly half-Portuguese Eurasian from Macao.

At night, we listened to and watched the South China Sea from the veranda as junkboat and sampan navies fought in the islands off Hong Kong, broadside to broadside and no quarter given, C.I.A.-armed pirates against PRC gunboats trying to sneak saboteurs and weapons into the colony.

It was all very exciting and terribly unique, I guess; but like so many expat kids I didn't really appreciate my reality. To me, the only place to be, the most exciting place, was Stateside, the U.S.A., a country I barely remembered and didn't comprehend at all. To me it was a magic kingdom, a shining scramble of Cowboys & Indians, *The Living Desert,* and Donald Duck and the Voodoo-Hoodoo Doll.

When we finally moved back to the United States, when I was eleven, it was to the East Coast, the dull-as-dust environs of Washington, D.C. Of course, I never felt at home there. My imagination soared west, out to where the deer and the antelope played and the skies were not cloudy all day, where the winds blew free and seldom was heard a discouraging word, if any at all. I survived by poring over maps that showed places like Teec Nos Pos, the Grand Canyon, the Snake River and the Growler Mountains (in my dreams, they actually *growled*). I read and re-read Jack Kerouac and nourished visions of Olph-like underground rivers, thudding tom-toms, turquoise mines, Diamonds as Big as the Ritz, and ghost towns populated by wise old white-whiskered Gabby Sages and, as my dreams entered adolescence, beautiful and concupiscent young women who danced to "Red River Rock" in black silk underwear and cowboy boots.

Well, at least one of the dreams came true—not a bad percentage, when you think about it.

When I finally escaped from prep school, with a highly conditional diploma, I immediately headed west, emulating my hero Kerouac by hitchhiking. But I didn't go quite far enough, looking back on it. I ended up at the University of Colorado, in Boulder, a place that was much more Ann Arbor or Yellow Springs, Ohio, than it was Deadwood or Snaketown, or the Ponderosa, for that matter.

I managed to rent a cabin up in the foothills for around a year and live something approaching the western life I had longed for as a kid: chopping firewood, sitting out blizzards snowed in for days on end, dealing with rural problems like rattlesnakes under the front porch, well water spiked with giardia, and stovepipe fires. But it was just a taste, a tantalizing whiff, of the Real Thing.

A dream deferred never dies; a vision on ice keeps forever.

In 1973, I finally made the move. I had just returned from the better part of a year traveling overland from Europe to India and Nepal, hanging out in Afghanistan, studying Buddhism in Dharmsala, walking to Everest in the monsoon. Back in Boulder, I missed getting married by a day; luckily, the bride got cold feet and fled. I was up in the air, feeling footloose but not really wanting that, longing for a home at last, a home that had never existed. Why not? My B.A. and master's degrees in social anthropology weren't exactly flinging open the doors of opportunity. I had written a novel, which for good reasons no one had wanted to publish. I had, in short, the special freedom that comes with an almost complete dearth of opportunity.

When a friend told me about this town called Telluride, named after a kind of ore they mined there, a conglomeration of gold, silver, lead, zinc, and copper, I said to myself, This is it. I packed up my $600 '64 VW bus, cashed out my meager savings, and headed west again.

The Telluride I moved to was just coming out of an era of near ghost-townhood, the bottoming-out bust phase of the old boom-and-bust cycle. There was a tiny ski area, open less than a year; the mine at the dead end of the valley was going twenty-four hours a day, ferreting wealth out of the mysterious depths of the mountains, riding a temporary upsurge in metals prices. There was just enough happening, in other words, to support a smallish wave of immigration: of people like me.

Just enough, but not too much: it was still the West I had read and fantasized about when I was a kid, years ago. Bighorns still grazed the peaks overlooking the northern edge of town; during the harshest blizzards they would take refuge on the rooftops of Main Street, waiting there for the weather to break. There were bears in the garbage cans every fall, fattening up for the long winter hibernation. Wolves and wolverines are officially extinct in Colorado, but according to locals both species could be found around Telluride, in obscure environs like Deer Trail Basin, along with a race of coyotes white as snow that roamed the high basins.

Then there were the local human beings. Right through the 1950s the town had sported a wild-hair outlaw economy, with brothels, bootleggers, and gambling houses. To get the hootch to market past the cops, the distillers reportedly took it into the mine through the Telluride portal and out the other side on the far end of the mountain, around Ouray. From there it was an easy run to the thirsty hordes in Montrose, Durango, Gunnison, Junction.

"To-hell-you-ride," the pious prudes in the nearby lowlands called the town.

Things hadn't changed all that much when I got there in '73. Some folks packed guns, Saturday Night specials and hogleg .44s, to the Elks Club dances. In a few years the new generation of locals would get into the spirit of things all too well, and a popular song called "Smugglers' Blues," romanticizing the grungy world of cocaine, would contain the line "They hide it up in Telluride—."

Once you got to know them, the old miners would wink, chuckle, and tell of their exploits in "high-grading." When times were tough, or the miners were just more cheesed off than usual at Newmont Mining, the gigantic multinational octopus that owned the mine, newly discovered veins of rich, high-grade gold ore would somehow go unreported to the company. Instead, the hardrock crew who discovered the lode would surreptitiously clean out the whole thing, smuggling the loot out over a period of days or even weeks in their big steel lunchboxes.

Shortly after moving to Telluride, I found myself talking with a grizzled, rock dust–drused miner in the Sheridan Bar.

"Ya ever see a man carrying sixty pounds of ore in his lunchbox and trying to make it look like it's empty? Sweat poppin' out on his face and his hand about to come off at the wrist? Har har har!"

The old-timers loved telling their stories to any newcomer who'd listen.

Once or twice a year shady characters would come to town and set up shop in the back rooms of saloons with assay kits, scales, and wallets full of cash; when they left, they had with them the community's whole stash of high grade, of nuggets, dust, and crudely refined lumps of near-pure gold.

This wasn't ancient history, far from it; high-grading was still going on when I moved to Telluride.

"Buy me another round," the old-timer said, "and I'll tell you more."

WA-HOO!! I loved it.

It wasn't just Telluride, it was the whole San Juans, the whole southwestern corner core of the Rockies.

A friend of mine, call him Joe, had just moved to one of the San Juans' slightly-lower-in-altitude ranching towns when a group of leathery little stockmen in big hats came up to him on Main Street.

"You that new feller? Come with us."

They led Joe into a white frame house just off Main. A man was sitting in a chair in the middle of the living room. He was dead, due to the fact that most of his head was missing.

"That's Shorty Rogers," the spokesman for the cowboys said. "He's dead. And we're the coroner's jury. We're appointing you foreman."

Joe looked at the dead man and then walked through the house, followed by his fellow jurors. They found a hunting rifle lying on the floor in the kitchen; it smelled like it had been fired recently. Nobody said a word. Joe used a rag from the sink to pick up the rifle and carry it back into the living room.

He looked around at his companions. "Well, why don't you tell me what you think happened?" There was an immediate piping chorus:

"Suicide."

"Looks lak suicide to me."

"Kilt himself, I reckon."

"Hmm. I'm not so sure," Joe said. "First of all, how come we found the gun in the kitchen?"

The old guys all looked at each other. "Someone musta moved it," one of them volunteered.

"And second—" Joe held the muzzle of the gun to the remains of Shorty's jaw and took the dead man's arm and stretched it to-

8

ward the trigger. It didn't reach, not by a long shot. "—how'd he pull the trigger?"

A long moment of uncomfortable glances between the "jurors."

"Mebbe he used a stick," suggested one old coot.

"So where's the stick?"

"Whoever moved the gun stole the stick."

"Why do you think Shorty mighta killed himself?" Joe asked.

"Because he felt guilty about stealin' our cattle all these years," one old man grunted. Everyone else nodded.

Joe looked around at the coroner's jury. They were all avoiding his gaze studiously. A sudden realization struck him: the jury had killed Shorty.

Well, if you're going to move someplace, you can't start out raising a bunch of trouble.

"Makes sense to me," Joe said. "I find for death by suicide!"

The room seemed to deflate from a great exhalation of relief.

"You know something?" the spokesman for the jurors said, grinning. "You're gonna fit in around here jist fine. Now let's go see what they're serving at the cafe. Lunch is on us."

Ah, wilderness, of every kind and variety.

That first year, a friend of mine was night-hiking down the grassy ski trails on Coonskin by midsummer moonlight. He came around a corner, and did a colossal double take—a mountain lion was crouched less than eighty feet away, feasting on a just-slain bull elk. A BIG mountain lion, an alpha male the size of a Harley-Davidson, with canine teeth like railroad spikes. The great eyes gazed back at him, unblinking and aglow, like the light

9

leaking from a nuclear reactor core. *Chomp crunch crack chomp:* the jaws that could crack a baseball bat in half like a breadstick noshed on elk tartare, washing it down with quarts of hot blood.

Like most of us early-seventies pilgrims my friend was an urbanite, a refugee from the cities and campuses of Colorado's Front Range and beyond. He had come to Telluride partly due to some vague idea of becoming a Mountain Man, Jeremiah Johnson or Grizzly Adams with a chain saw and a Jeep. But at moments like this, eyeball to eyeball with two hundred pounds of Ravenous Reaper, it was pretty hard to maintain the image.

My friend crept down along the edge of the forest, shaking like a quakey. Every footstep seemed to take an eternity; the lights of town below looked like they were on a different planet. At last, when the mountain lion was lost to view behind him, concealed by the steep angle of the mountain and the timber, he took off like a rocket. Several tumbles, ankle twists, belly flops, and face plants later he hit the base of the mountain at full tilt, forded the San Miguel River, turned east on Pacific, and arrived at the old Senate Bar, nearly taking the swinging doors off their hinges and landing on a bar stool in a cloud of dust.

The barkeep eyed him up and down. "What'll it be?"

"Crown Royal and a Currs chaser. And keep 'em coming."

The barkeeper slammed the bottle and the shot glass down in front of him on the bar. He tried to pick them up, but his hands were shaking too hard.

"Would you mind pouring 'em down my throat while you're at it? Just the first round. I can handle it from there."

* * *

Well, I was in the lost heart of the Rockies, all right. And really, life there was lived on a different scale—bigger, harder, grander. It took some getting used to.

How about the big tramp logger from just north of here who cut his hand clean off at the wrist when his monster Husqvarna chain saw hit an iron-hard knot and jumped sideways?

He was living with his six-year-old son, Mattock, and his wife . . . well, she run off with some slick sumbitch from Vail. He and his son were living in an unheated tin trailer the size of a one-car garage up a long dirt road; he was home-schooling the boy with a Bible and an old *Worldbook Encyclopedia* with half the pages eaten out by pack rats.

The boy was inside, reading "Whales," when the accident happened. The first thing the logger did was, he picked up his severed hand, dusted it off, and put it in his jacket pocket. Then he staunched the stump with a compression bandage, an old wadded-up Coors T-shirt anchored with electrician's tape.

Making sure his wound was concealed, thrusting the bandaged lump into his jacket pocket along with the dead hand because he didn't want to scare the boy, he went into the trailer.

"Yo, Mattock . . ."

"Yes, Daddy?" The little silver-towhead looked up with lambent blue eyes from a favorite photograph of a Pacific grey whale breaching, airborne like some kind of wondrous marine dirigible.

"Need you to run down the road to Hooper's. If Miz Hooper's there, have her run her pickup up here. I need a quick ride to town."

"Jimmy's not workin'?" Jimmy was the woodcutter's ancient GMC, bought with 337,512 miles on it for $175 at a Forest Service auction, and it was always crapping out.

"Yep, Jimmy's feelin' kinda under the weather. If Miz Hooper ain't home, try Saunders." The real reason the logger didn't drive himself, of course, was that he couldn't work the steering wheel and the stick on the winding roads with only one hand.

"OK, Daddy. Be back quicker'n a flea." The boy pulled on his laceless thrift store sneakers and flew out the door. He didn't suspect a thing. To him, his father was as indestructible as the granite mountains that overlooked the little trailer in its clearing.

When his son was gone, the woodcutter poured himself a glass of spring water with his good hand and slowly drank it. He washed his face and battened his unruly hair down with more water, and ran a comb through it. He thought about changing into a clean shirt for the hospital but decided not to; he only had three shirts, and he didn't want to get blood all over one. He realized suddenly that he was feeling weak. His head felt like it was tethered to the rest of his body by the thinnest of twines, that at any moment it might break loose and float away. And then what would happen?

"Sweet Jesus, protect me and my son Mattock in this our hour of need," he said under his breath. He poured some Western Family honey onto a piece of bread, ate it, and immediately felt strength. He made sure he had his wallet: you needed wallets when you went to hospitals and such, even if the wallet contained just two five-dollar bills and no insurance card.

The last thing he did was he went out back to the outhouse and took himself a big, serious crap. He'd heard that when they put you under, knocked you out, you sometimes lost control of your body, and he wasn't about to crap in his pants in front of a bunch of strangers. Part pride, part politeness.

He cleaned himself up carefully with his one good hand, and then went back out front and sat on the trailer steps, waiting for Mattock to bring Miz Hooper or one of the Saunderses back. He found himself grinning, despite the grinding pain.

He shook hands with himself in his pocket, warm live hand and cold dead one. "Glad to meet you, Jack Dix. Heard a lot about you. Nothin' bad, I hope? Nothin' too bad. Well, I try to do my best . . ."

Then he just sat there. Breathing in the sweet nude scent of cut pine, his ears filled with the whirring sussuration of the quakey grove in the breeze, the million silver leaves, the heat-hazy ridges of conifer stretching away to a skyline of stone peaks with patches of old snow. One was the shape of an elephant, he thought, but missin' its butt, like somebody shot it off. And there was an angel, but with only one wing, and a tiny itty-bitty head . . . but if you were an angel, why'd you need a brain, any-how?

Miz Hooper showed up, and they dropped Mattock off with her two kids, eleven-year-old Astra and nine-year-old Chapar-ral, on the way down to town. When they were alone in the car and Jack told her what had happened, she stared at him with great owl eyes, her slim, worn, sundark face suddenly bloodless and pale. "Jack Dix, you've got to take care of yourself," she said finally.

"Yeah," Jack grinned. "Whoever heard of a one-armed wood-cutter?"

The local doc put the hand on ice and helicoptered him and it up to St. Mary's in Junction, where the Experts successfully put him back together again. The old hand felt funny, strange, at first, but it slowly got better.

When he came home from Grand Junction, Miz Hooper had organized a benefit for him, to help pay the astronomical hospital bills. A band called the Rude Boyzs, friends of Crazy Vince, played for free. They turned out to be a Hopi reggae group, but nobody much minded. There was also a potluck, and a Chinese auction, and Miz Hooper sold one of her new weavings for $440—though she could've got twice that in Santa Fe—and kicked that in, too.

As night fell, they lit shopping-bag candelarias, and Jack and Miz Grace Hooper ended up awkwardly slow-dancing to "Many Rivers to Cross" in the grass and wildflowers behind the church, as meteors crisscrossed the skies above.

The Lay of the Land

A brief word about this landscape of ours.

The San Juan Mountains and vicinity have got to be the most twisted, convoluted, cantankerous, crumpled, moiled, roiled, rugosity-rife, paradoxical, and one-step-forward-three-steps-back terrain the Great Spirit Wakan-tonka, along with plate tectonics, sedimentation, erosion, vulcanism, salt dome collapse, and what-all, ever conspired to create.

There is a certain surreality to it, you might say.

It is anchored near its south end by the silliest "place" ever anointed: Four Corners National Monument, "the only point where four states meet in one spot." Ah, yes. Like the Highest Point in Iowa, or the Continental Center of the United States,

Four Corners lacks something in drama when you actually get there.

Over there is Arizona: sandstone, sand, and brush. And over there is New Mexico: sandstone, sand, and brush. And over there is Utah: s., s., and b. And over there is Colorado . . . well, you get the picture.

Thirty-seven degrees north by, um, a smidgen less than 109 degrees west . . . the "place" isn't even a good abstraction! But the U.S. Park Service has placed a giant sort of plaque there, set in the ground, surrounded by a parking lot and rest rooms, a demi-oasis so the Winnebago crowd can stop there like lemmings as they traverse what they see as mere Emptiness. It's a great boon to the local Navajos, who erect a sprawling bazaar there every tourist season, flogging cheap carpets, jewelry, and such. If you're lucky, when you drop by, someone will be selling mutton stew and fry bread, along with cold sodas.

In years past it was a custom among archaeologists, river runners, and other bedrock characters to pose for nude photos atop the center of the monument at dusk or dawn, when no one else was around. Alas, I have lost the only one I ever took, of a big-bummed, nineteen-year-old improper Bostonian archaeologist with whom I excavated at Mesa Verde one summer: she was grinning saucily back over her shoulder, glowing like a pale pink rose in flagrante delicto, in the sunset.

But back to the physical truths of the country.

First, at the center of everything, my own San Juans. Serious summits, brooding monsters like Redcloud, Sunshine, Wetterhorn, El Diente (the Fang), Sneffels, Shandoka (Storm Maker), all these and more in the 14,000-foot-plus category, plus literally hundreds of lesser but equally imperious peaks. Almost none of the San Juan peaks are of the "walk-up" variety; most require a rope and/or a modicum of moxie to scale. In the summer, thunderstorms grumble and lightning slashes on sheer crags, crumbling arêtes and steep scree slopes as dodgy as a greased slate roof. Watch it, pilgrim! In the winter, these stone giants wrap themselves in robes of snow and storm, aloof and otherworldly, and shrug off the unwary with the biggest avalanches in the Lower Forty-eight.

When the first surveyors came through here in the late 1800s, the intrepid Gardiner and company, the peaks bore yet another peril: many of the highest ones were inhabited in the summer by king-sized grizzly bears, eager to vary their diet of elk, berries, groundhogs and gophers, grass and leaves, with a laggard geographer or two. More than once the mapmakers had to grab theodolites and transits and run for their lives.

The miners and ranchers systematically slaughtered the big bears, of course, in the San Juans and the rest of the state. The last officially recorded Colorado griz, an emaciated, weary old sow, was slain back in '79 just north of Durango, and since then the subspecies has been on the Extinct List. But recently credible reports of new griz sightings have emerged from the South San Juans, way down by the New Mexico line.

A few years ago, a veteran wrangler was riding fence on an old Spanish land grant ranch in the nethermost South San Juans, on the New Mexico line. He tells it this way:

"I tied my horse to a tree and sat down to eat an apple, when a couple of big bears came out of the woods. They looked like full-grown adult black bears, but then they started to play together like cubs. I just couldn't figure it out . . . till the MOTHER came into sight. She was a giant. My hair stood on end. I was at the top of a coupla-hundred-yard slope, steep as a cow's face—yeah, nothing for a full-grown griz to run up before you could move. She smelled me, too, and she didn't like it—she reared up on her hind legs and kept sniffing the air. I didn't move a muscle. Finally, she turned and cuffed her cubs back into the woods."

A big black bear with a brown coat? Blacks can come in a whole rainbow of shades, from blue to red to russet to brown. "No way," says the wrangler. "I've seen black bears too many times to count. She wasn't only a griz, she was a big one." And I believe him, without a shred of a doubt.

Three cheers, say I, for the San Juans, where even the griz survives! It's a miracle as glorious as the reappearance of the coelacanth, or if someday a great auk came paddling up onto a New Zealand beach and laid an egg the size of a rugby ball in the sand. I don't necessarily want to meet a San Juan griz face to face, but I sure like thinking, knowing, they're out there.

Between the peaks run cold rivers and streams like the Uncompahgre (Stinky River to the Utes, because of sulphur springs near its headwaters), the San Miguel (Telluride, my town, lies athwart its headwaters), the Dolores (River of Sorrows), the Animas (River of Souls), and La Plata (Silver), on their way to join the mighty Colorado and San Juan rivers. Along their devious way, they and their tributaries cut mazes of mountain ravines and desert gorges, a Through-the-Looking-Glass landscape where a ridge or a rimrock can seem close enough to touch and take three days to get to . . . if you can get there at all. Like I said, check the map. It's a jigsaw mess, a glorious one.

Unfortunately, parts of our rivers and streams have been shamefully ruined by the pork-barrel plumbers of the Bureau of Wreck-the-Nation, often comparatively recently. When I moved down to the San Juans, for instance, the Uncompahgre flowed from Ridgway north to Montrose through a series of lovely old family ranches (Cookie Tree was my favorite). Now the valley and its ranches have been drowned, by a dam and an ugly reservoir whose supposed purpose is to provide power for a future "industrial boom" in the sleepy little town of Montrose, where the heaviest industry is a chocolate-covered cherries factory. And, of course, there's "recreation." You can trudge around the fake lake on one of those grim loop trails the U.S. government is so fond of, or you can fish—but remember, the (factory) trout are so loaded with heavy metals from upstream mine dumps that you eat them at your peril.

Another liquid jewel, the Upper Dolores River, has also been flooded out since I moved to the San Juans, at a reservoir just outside the town of Dolores. Look fast, pilgrim, there goes Paradise! Yep, recreation again, plus water to irrigate the pinto bean farms on the high mesas south of the river.

These perjured waters descend from the mountains through mesas and plateaus on their way to the deserts of New Mexico, Arizona, Utah. This intermediate mesa zone, too, is righteously empty, and equally grand. We've got elbowroom to burn. In fact, Emptiness is our Most Important Product, I'd say. Sailboat fuel. Nada thing.

Telluride is the seat of San Miguel County, a long, thin county that starts out in the east atop the lofty San Juans and descends on and on and on, all the way to the slickrock and sand of the Utah border. A big county, and still without a single traffic light.

The West End of the county is truly No Man's Land. Dry Creek Basin, Disappointment Valley, Paradox Valley: sandstone ramparts, rolling veldts, abandoned mines, two-lane blacktop rolling on and on—watch for range cattle at night—and dirt roads to nowhere. Locals used to regularly see flying saucers out here in the seventies.

The old Norwood town doc used to fly around at night in his Cessna, chasing renegade discs down and photographing them. Cattle mutilations? You bet.

The very names out in this Interzone bespeak the sheer goofiness of the terrain. The Paradox Valley, for example, is a long, deep valley bounded on both sides by cliffs hundreds of feet high. It must have a stream running down it, right? Or maybe even a river? Nope. Nothing runs down the middle of the Paradox. It wasn't cut, see, like any normal valley; instead, it formed when a vast salt bed far beneath the sandstone somehow collapsed. Or so the geologists say.

Disappointment Valley got its name from the pioneers: like Paradox, it looks like it should, must, contain a watercourse of some size, at least a small river, at its middle. But it doesn't, just a seasonal creek. Disappointing, yes; especially if you're bone tired, covered with horse flies and dust, worried that a Ute sniper is getting ready to part your hair down to the cerebellum with a .44 slug, and your empty canteens clank disconsolately against your saddle.

The San Juan country has always been famous for its droughts . . . as well as massive snowpacks, meltoffs, cloudbursts, and flash floods. The same canyon kills you with thirst one day, drowns you the next, and then freeze-dries what's left for posterity.

Yep, we got The Map, podner; ours is nonpareil. Second to none in its ornery delights.

There's that town way down south of the Dolores River, in the most distant reaches of San Miguel County. What's in a name? In this case, the burg's founders proudly christened it Range: Ya-hoo, yippi-ki-yi-yay! That is, till the U.S. Postal Service informed them there already was a Range somewhere else in Colorado, so the San Miguel County version was disallowed.

Imagine the weeping and lamentation, the rending of breasts and the tearing of tresses. I see in my mind's laughing eye those saddle mutts exclaiming, "Consarn it," and worse in their whiney drawls, punting their hats out the window or stomping them into ruin while the womenfolk sing "Oh God Our Help in Ages Past." "Range" was perfect, so perfect, in fact, that they eventually decided if they couldn't have it forwards, they'd have it backwards: EGNAR!

That's my home, my habitat, all right.

The Goldsworthy Shack

My first real home in the San Juans was a tarpaper sheepherders' shack next to a little oblong lake on the lonesome road from Telluride south toward New Mexico. Nine thousand, five hundred feet above sea level, perched between the two headwaters of the San Miguel River on Turkey Creek Mesa, in a stand of quakies.

There was a dirt road to the place, but in winter the road was blocked by snow and you had to ski or snowshoe in. The cabin was tiny, a single room with a ladder leading to a loft. You could just barely stand up in the center of the loft, with its sloping A-framed roof.

The place belonged to Cecil Goldsworthy and his family, old-time Welsh miners who'd been in the Telluride area since the last century. They had allowed it to slide into dilapidation and were happy when I offered to rent it for $75 a month.

I moved in with my friend Holly just before the first snowfall of '73, after a frantic round of repairs: nailing the metal roofing back down, stuffing fiberglass insulation panels into the hollow walls, installing a wood-burning heater and a propane tank for the beat stove. I had four cords of fresh-cut aspen hauled in and dumped by the front door and had just finished digging an out-house hole back in the woods and sticking a one-holer sitdown toilet over it when the first big snow hit. I never did put a roof over it or walls around it: it remained a defecatory version of Han Shan's famous Zen "house" in the Cold Mountain Poems:

> Cold Mountain is a house . . .
> The east wall beats on the west wall,
> At the center nothing.

Except in this case, "At the center, a poor devil with a blue butt sitting there freezing to death."

As the snow plummeted down that first night, flakes the size of postage stamps, we lit the three kerosene lamps that illuminated the place and stoked up the stove with split shanks of aspen. The wood heater roared like a dragon, consuming a bellyful of logs within an hour. Soon the cabin was so hot we had to open the door to keep from parboiling.

An owl hooted somewhere on the wooded slope above the shack and the lake: hunting season. They hoot and hoot till some small rodent, hiding underground or under snow, bristling and aquiver with terror, makes a break for it. Then they drop from the treetops without a sound (the owl's wings are specially designed for this) and—KWATZU!—in a split Zen instant you're an ex-rodent about to be transmogrified into Owlness.

It seemed perfect at the time, of course, living in the heart of the mountains, in Nature's shining core . . . splitting logs, melting snow for water, skiing out to the old VW bus to drive to town, reading by the golden glow of kerosene. But let me tell you, those scenes from *Never Cry Wolf,* where the snowbound biologist is being dripped on and then frozen, then dripped on again, besieged by mice and woodrats, his nut cracked by too many howling winds and whiteouts out the window—they have a lot more to do with the truth than anything Rousseau or Ernest (Ecotopia) Callenbach ever dreamed, and I do mean dreamed, up.

Not to mention Charlie Chaplin snowbound in *The Gold Rush.* Charlie's partner, a bearded leviathan, hallucinates that Charlie is a roast chicken and chases him around the cabin. Hilarious, but less so if you've ever wintered in the mountains. And don't forget Alferd Packer, the Colorado Cannibal, of the Donner party in the Sierra Nevada. No wonder the Utes, whose mountains these actually are, avoided winter up here, migrating to the lower valleys and mesas during the snow months. They knew better.

Of course, we were just minutes from the paved road, and maybe seven miles from town. But distance is relative, the higher you go. Turkey Creek Mesa, where the Goldsworthy shack sat, was virtually unpopulated back then. When the roads were icy, and you had to begin every journey to the outside world by skiing to a cold and cranky old car; when you came home, it was to a freezing meat locker of a domicile . . . well, you felt like you were living on the dark side of the moon.

"Going bushy," they call it up in Alaska. The consequence of living too much on your own, too far out from the edge of the humanity. It's a slow and stately downhill procession of asocial decisions. Like, why shave? Why not wear the same turtleneck for a week? Mm-hmm, let's heat up that hamburger hash again, it's only five days old! Leak in the roof? Put a bucket under it. More leaks? Buy more buckets.

By spring, life was a total mess. My woman was gone, and the old van was out to throw a rod. Field mice besieged the cabin: every night I awoke to the snap of a trap and a terminal scrabble and yeep as another tiny being bit the steel. It did not make for golden slumbers. Bloody awakenings, bloody nightmares. There was too much snow to hike and not enough to ski. BLARGH!! One March blizzard that year went on for nine days straight without a glimpse of the sun. So I fled to the beaches of Mexico, and when I returned I moved into my attorney's storeroom.

Hardrock Days

I'm a miner, I'm a mucker,
I'm a mean motherfucker,
And I work down in the Idarado Mine . . .
                    —old Telluride miner's song

The mines were such a part of Telluride that I don't regret my brief (two months?) tenure at the Pandora Mine, aka Idarado, masquerading as a welder in the equipment dumps around the towering mill building.

It's nice to be a part, however small, of History. Plus I needed the money. History schmistory.

I can't say it was a great job. In point of fact, it was one of the worst I ever had, in a long and checkered blue-collar career of bad jobs that included bobcat, jackhammer, and tractor operator on the Front Range, woodpecker on a Maryland fence crew, etc., etc. Telluride is where the Wobblies' mining union was broken early in the century, with vigilantes, forced deportations, and assassinations, and that dark legacy clung to the Idarado. Owned by Newmont Mining, a huge multinational headed by a shadowy figure named something like Aristotle Azimov, Idarado paid poorly, treated its employees like peons, and was dangerous to boot.

Dickens would have dug the place.

I got a good taste of mine work Newmont style at my orientation talk from the gloomy foreman who hired me. "First thing you gotta do is, go to the hardware store in town and buy yourself a hardhat and a pair of steeltoe mucking boots."

"And you guys pay for that, right?"

"Nope. Now, your shift starts at eight A.M."

"So I should show up a few minutes early?"

"Nope. You be there at the mill twenty minutes before work, when that first whistle blows. Be ready to go in your work clothes when the second whistle blows, at eight."

"So I guess I don't get paid for those first twenty minutes."

"Nope. And don't go to town for lunch—ya bring your own lunch and eat it here."

"Reason being—?"

"Reason is, folks in town don't want ta see a bunch of dirty miners in town for their lunch break. And you work till the first afternoon whistle at five—then you change out of your mining clothes on your own time. Any problems with that?"

"Nope."

Ah, the Idarado. The working conditions were something out of the Smithsonian Museum of Science and Industry, or present-day Siberia. For instance: The Crusher, a hopper the size of a huge closet that mashed big cobblestones and small boulders into something like gravel, and lacked a proper safety switch. One time it got jammed, and the operator shut it off and climbed down into it to clear the obstruction. Along came a foreman, who saw the machine wasn't running, didn't notice his fellow-proletarian down in there, and . . . yep, he turned it back on.

And then there was the old pickup truck with no brakes, crewed by two ancient men, whose job it was to drive high up into the basins overlooking the mine entrance periodically, up skinny switchbacked goat roads, check the lofty portals, openings, and stopes on the naked stone slopes, and then return. Descent was achieved by a combination of expert downshifting and heavy use of the creeper gear . . . and sheer luck. This system worked, until one day as the two neared the bottom of the mountain, the truck ran out of gas. It careered down the last pitch of steep road, slam-banged across a tailings pile, and crash-landed in a tailings pond.

And so on.

Of course, I was there only eight weeks, two autumnal months, cutting up scrap metal in the junkyard behind the mill and welding weird pieces of metal to other weird pieces of metal to make bigger weird pieces of metal, which were then inspected and hauled away by the foreman to be used for God knows what. My friend Jardine got twenty-five cents more an hour and worked underground, blasting out ore and timbering hazardous shafts and tunnels. He ended up quitting and fleeing, all the way to Hong Kong, where he became an international banker.

The Idarado is closed down, along with all the other mines in the San Juans. And, funny thing, what they've left behind is a feeling of sadness, of loss. Time has that gift. The grievous wrongs of the past mellow out and lose their edge until they ultimately disappear, leaving a faux-golden tableaux with a faux-golden glow. Or perhaps not false. Maybe just the uneasy truce between past and present that contains, someplace inside, the one real true Truth.

In 1990, I go back out to the Pandora portal of the Idarado to check in with the last of the old crew—seven guys, all that's left of the thousands of Swedes, Finns, Welshmen and Irish, Navajos, Utes and Mexicans, Mitteleuropeans, and Transylvanian trolls who passed through those troglodyte vaults. There's no actual mining going on anymore, just these hardcore veterans of the underground, keeping the equipment running, replacing rotting timbers, pumping out flooded chambers, and another five Idarado employees on the other side of the mountain, at the Camp Bird portal, keeping things functioning there.

I barely knew them when I worked here; they were the Serious Masters, after all, while I was unwilling, unknowing, and uncaring. But here they are, the Magnificent Seven of the Idarado. George Cappis, sixty-eight, quiet, lanky, distinguished in a Jimmy Stewart kind of way. Tough and taciturn Joe Smart. Wry Jerry Heldman, master mechanic ("George breaks the machinery, I fix it," he laughs). Chief chemist Larry Stevens, who could play a cowboy hero in a western, no doubt about it. Sawed-off and rock-hard Jerry Albin. Kindly, stout Francis Warner. The sly, crackerjawed old Welshman Cecil Goldsworthy.

All of these men were born and raised in Colorado, and Goldsworthy, Albin, and Warner were all actually born in Telluride. Except for Francis, who was the town's fire chief for several years, all these guys have worked at Idarado for at least seventeen years. For some, mining is a family tradition. One of Cappis's brothers and two of Goldsworthy's, along with several of Warner's uncles, worked in the mine in earlier years. Larry Stevens's father, Dick, was plant superintendent at the mine for forty-five years.

Rock runs in the blood here. As does pride. "The old miners we learned from, they were amazing," says Albin. "They knew everything. They belonged to the Old Days, when the miners around here could do anything themselves: wiring, timbering, blasting, geology. There's no one like that around today. Those times are gone forever."

Maybe so, but the seven men at the Idarado have managed to preserve a lot of the skills. Jerry Heldman, for instance, is a master on the lathe, machine-tooling parts and cutting and threading pipes with a watchmaker's finesse, shaving cold steel down to a 64th of an inch while joking with his partners over his shoulder. Larry Stevens spreads out a whole range of unrefined and refined ore samples on his office tabletop: high-grade glittering with flakes of native gold, hefty hunks of rock dark and heavy with silver, a big button-shaped piece of semirefined metal, 90 percent gold and 10 percent silver, that makes the greed juices flow in the corners of your mouth despite yourself. Where's his wizard's hat? He's wearing a John Deere baseball cap!

It's the alchemy of the mill. And it's all about time. "In June, I'll have put in fifty years out here," Cappis says. "And in October, Gay [his wife, the much-beloved birdlike little county clerk] and I will be celebrating our fiftieth wedding anniversary. We couldn't afford to get married until I got on at the mine and saved up all my money for five months." Back then, the mine portal was high above its present site, and the men rode a tram up to work. The day the Idarado's Pandora portal was opened is etched in concrete by the entrance: 1945.

Get these characters talking, and the stories start coming.

"In the winter of 1947," someone recounts, "muskrats would swim in, following the drainage ditches. We used to feed 'em."

"And remember the beaver that came swimming into the hoist room? He was just lookin' for a home." Laughter. "We roped him and put him in the cart next to the motor to keep him warm. When the hoist man saw him, he climbed up on his bench—he thought that beaver was gonna eat him! We got that old beaver out of the mine and turned him loose in the crick."

"It must have been pretty dangerous down there," I interject, remembering the mishaps I heard about during my brief tenure in the mine dumps above ground.

They all shake their heads no. "The most dangerous job was driving the ore trucks down the canyon when it was icy."

But then they start recollecting. "Well, there was the time when that fella got caught between the ore cart and the side of the tunnel."

"What happened?"

"Oh, he got crushed to death."

"And how about when so-and-so was riding an ore cart and didn't see that low-hanging timber."

"Was he hurt?"

"Well, yeah, you might say that. He was decapitated."

The stories start coming, thick and fast. Like, you would set off dynamite in a stope full of loose rock and muck, and while you crouched in your doghole (an emergency chamber in the side of the tunnel) boulders would roll by, big ones, thirty feet on a side. There were other stopes you would blast, and nothing would happen. Bad news. The rocks were jammed up, and you had to poke at them from your doghole, to try and get them to cut loose. When they did, if you weren't fast you could be buried alive.

Some sections of the mine were insanely unstable. One miner working alone on a remote rock face went to check on the air hose of his pneumatic drill, and when he returned to where he was working, a section of roof a hundred feet long and fifteen feet thick had fallen. If he had been there—

"What did he do then?" I asked foolishly.

"He got the hell out of there!" Laughter like a rock might laugh.

"When did he go back to work?"

"Never. He got himself a job above ground, with the town."

But they insist mining's the best life a man could choose. "There's nothing else like it," says Goldsworthy. "Like the variety," Albin adds. And then delivers the punchline: "One day you could be mining, the next day you could be pushing up grass."

But they're serious, this craggy hardbitten crew, serious romantics.

"In the winter some of the high portals would fill up with ice a mile deep; they wouldn't thaw out till fall, and then they'd start filling up again."

"Remember that Navajo medicine man worked down there awhile? He'd gather crystals and grind 'em up at home to use in his sand paintings."

"One time we found a room that was all crystals, floors, ceiling, walls. It was half filled with water. Lit up by miners' lamps . . . like magic."

"What happened to it?"

"What happened to it? We sealed it up again, and kept working the vein we were following. It's still down there."

Childlike wonder still on their faces, at the memory.

"In the mines, you'll never know everything there is to know," says Francis Warner.

"There are still big veins down there, that have never been followed to the end. Way, way down there," says Albin dreamily.

It was a strange and unequaled realm, no doubt about it, as otherworldly and wondrous as the Gnome King Ruggedo's kingdom in the *Wizard of Oz*. Oz . . . an oz. of silver, an oz. of gold. . . .

Today, of course, the mine is still closed. I ran into Jerry Albin three summers ago buckarooing an ATV over a high snow-packed saddle up above La Junta Basin, still keeping an eye on those high portals and openings in the very heights of the mountains. Francis Warner died in an auto accident a few years back. We all miss him.

Deep in their hearts, the mountains hold their secrets.

The Sweetest Time

"The sweetest time is just before the revolution," someone once said. Well, when it comes to boomtowns, the sweetest time comes just before the boom.

My first few years in T'ride, when the ski area was barely making it and you could still buy a Victorian on Colorado Avenue for twenty thousand bucks, were ineffable times. Think of Aspen in the fifties, Paris in the thirties, or Kathmandu in the sixties. Everything hung in barely balanced equipoise, breathtakingly friable, excruciatingly rarefied. I think we were unconscious at the time of just how precious this high dream-aerie of ours was: how precious, and how mortal. A freeze-dried edition of *One Hundred Years of Solitude*, bursting with strangeness, sorrow, and ecstasy and frail as a frost blossom.

There were fireflies on the lawns in town then, weren't there? Or am I imagining that particular bit of magic? But the bats, they were very real, pirouetting through the summer streetlight haloes. And families of skunks would cross the street on a July evening, mother in front, single file of young nose to tail behind, vanishing into the perforated foundations of this or that old miner's shack or shed. Golden eagles nested high above the mine mill, in the lofty tops of dead pine trees. Rainbows, dirt roads, thunderheads, gods in the mist . . . we felt like we lived at the very edge of the Known World, or maybe even Beyond. When we went down to Montrose or Cortez to shop, the flatland locals would eye us up and down and snicker nervously. No law in Telluride. No order in Telluride. Craziness up there. Weirdness up there.

It wasn't just us new psychedelicized longhairs. The Telluride Reputation went back a long, long time. There were brothels in Telluride into the 1950s. The last town madame was an imposing dreadnought named Big Billie, who could knock an unruly miner out with one blow of the flat of her hand. Bootlegging and illegal gambling were always part of the scene, as were vengeance and payback outside the law. "Well, he needed killing" until recently was an all-purpose explanation that covered many an unsolved disappearance and death.

Dig under the cribs, the little whorehouses in the southeast corner of town under Coonskin, and you found empty bottles with LAUDANUM, MORPHINE, OPIUM in raised letters on the glass, left by Good-Time Girls who never ever had a good time. You found accounts in yellowing mining-era papers stuffed for insulation into the walls of old shacks: "Three bacchantes at the local Music Hall, wearying of their young but soiled lives, elected to seek their final release in the arms of the Chinaman's Morpheus last Saturday late, and alas were found too late by friends. Two names are confirmed: Canadian Lilly West, a half-breed Peigsan from that land to the north, and a local girl, Molly Fitshugh. Third and youngest was the little red-haired gal newly arrived at the Pick & Gad and very popular we are told with the customers, known only as 'Sloan'—"

Sometimes life there in Paradise was just plain funny. Like the time one of the TV networks was broadcasting a much-bally-hooed Shakespearean play, *Macbeth*, or maybe *Othello*, with Olivier, a crumb of Culture tossed to the nation's smartasses. A bunch of us New Telluridians exulted, and planned a whole evening around it. People drove down from cabins and tepees, yurts and sheep shacks, and gathered at the house of a friend in town who owned a gigantic old TV set.

After a potluck dinner of vegan casseroles and twice-poached trout, elk stew, beans, home-baked bread and pies, and lots of vino, we all gathered in front of the box for our feast of culture. Back then Telluride was served by just one station, a nutball Grand Junction–based entity called XYZ that served up a pas-tiche of network shows culled from all three webs along with lo-cal fare. We tuned it in, adjusted the rabbit ears—the hour struck—we held our breaths, and—*voila!* There was one of XYZ's announcers, clad in a tuxedo, grinning from ear to ear. He looked like a sidekick from one of those singing cowboy movies of the forties and fifties—Happy, or Cookie, or Kansas, something like that.

"Now folks," he drawled, "we have a real special treat fer ya tonight!" Audible joy from the Telluride audience.

"Yep, we're interruptin' our regular schedule this evenin' fer a once-in-a-lifetime experience—so let me interdooce—"

And then the TV cut to a jerky film of a barge powered by an airplane engine, the kind of thing Gyro Gearloose or Rube Goldberg might contrive, chugging down a desert river—"CAT-FISH-FISHIN' ON THE SAN JUAN, WITH THE LEGENDARY CATFISH CHRISTENSEN AN' HIS JET-BOAT, THE RUPTURED GOONYBIRD—"

A barrage of curses, moans, and disbelieving laughter filled the room. One zealot ran to the phone, dialed up XYZ, and screeched obscenities at the station manager till the guy threatened to call the cops. Meanwhile, on the box, Christensen explained how catfish hunt food using their sense of smell. As he moulded disgusting-looking turdlets of rotting garbage and gradoo for bait he grinned into the camera and explained, "The smellier the better, folks! Better wear an ole shirt while yer doin' this, or the wife might not let ya back in the double-wide, ho ho ho!"

"Shakespeare Night" broke up early.

Such were the vicissitudes of life in a small, remote resort. Of course, something inside us secretly loved it all. This was life on a raw and epic scale, a slapstick opera in the sky.

If you didn't have a car, you had to hitchhike over Dallas Divide to Ridgway and pick up the bus, north to Montrose and GJ or south to Albuquerque, to even start to get to the Outside World. You could always fly, of course, but this was long before Telluride had an airport. Back then, you had to somehow get to Montrose, Cortez, or Grand Junction, and fly to Denver, and then go on from there.

Flying to and from Colorado's Western Slope was another adventure in and of itself. Frontier Airlines serviced us Western Slopers with a fleet of primitive Convair-580 turbo-props that put the adventure back in flying. The Convair-580s operated at a much lower altitude and slower speed than today's commuter aircraft. Galumphing along at 200 mph, skimming over the high passes and peaks, they seemed to hit every possible pocket of turbulence over western Colorado, and there were lots of them. Jokesters dubbed the 580 the Vomit Comet. The German actor Klaus Kinski was so terrified after a caroming Convair-580 flight from Denver to Montrose for the Telluride Film Festival that he refused to return to Denver on what he called the Killer Death Plane; a poor festival volunteer had to drive the gibbering Prometheus-wannabe eleven hours over the mountains to Denver to pick up his flight back to Germany.

I remember one notable Denver-to-Gunnison-to-Montrose flight, in spring. I was returning from the East Coast, and my flight from New York to Denver was three hours late. I thought I had missed my Montrose connection, but I reckoned without the unreliability of the Frontier Airlines fleet. My Convair-580 was still sitting on the runway when I arrived at the gate two hours after scheduled departure. The plane had broken down yet again, mechanical trouble in one engine and electrical hassles in the navigation system. Finally, the problems were fixed (supposedly), and we were cleared for takeoff.

By that time, a spring blizzard had rolled in over the Western Slope. We bucketed and bounced west, over the Front Range, out of the blue and into the black. By the time we reached the Continental Divide you couldn't see much of anything out the window, and what you could see you didn't really want to: swirling abysses of cloud, snow building up on the wings, an occasional high summit groping up out of the storm for us, like an outtake from *One of Our Aircraft Is Missing* or *Lost Horizon*.

The storm swallowed us whole, and soon it became clear that we were lost. The pilot came on the P.A. to say, "Well, folks, looks like that ol' navigation system's gone on the schnitz again." A pretty young woman tourist from New York, sitting across the aisle from me, burst into tears. And who could blame her?

We circled and circled endlessly through the terminal murk, roller-coasting from air pocket to air pocket, the wings flapping like the wings on a dilapidated Mechano-set bird, the fuselage creaking, groaning, and whining, extremely unencouraging sounds. By now even us hard-core Western Slopers were having trouble maintaining our John Wayne facades.

A malicious old rancher with a scorpion-in-plastic string-tie clip cracked loud jokes about death, dismemberment, and such, but our laughter sounded thin and insincere. The girl from New York redoubled her weeping.

When we finally emerged from the Void, we were over Blue Mesa Reservoir, forty miles on the wrong side of Gunnison. We backtracked, landed in the gathering dusk on a runway covered with a foot of snow, dumped a few passengers and bags, and then headed on toward our final destination, Montrose. Whereupon we promptly got lost again. The flight from Gunnison to Montrose normally took fifteen, twenty minutes. This time it took nearly an hour before we finally reemerged from the turbulent darkness way up north of Delta and doglegged south to our destination.

Then, of course, I had a ninety-minute drive on snowy, icy roads to get home to Telluride. During which I managed to hit a huge bull elk that emerged out of a snow squall like a phantom. The elk got up and walked away from it, but I had to replace the radiator a week later.

But that's what it was all about, wasn't it? Paradise by its very nature is inconvenient, elusive, intractable, and impractical. If they try to sell you a Paradise that ain't all that, they're lying.

And when Telluride got too easy, well, the magic started ever so slowly leaking away.

But back then . . .

One always seemed to be in love, or about to be in love. It was a feeling that something, someone wonderful was waiting for you on those dirt streets, or on the trails—snow in winter, dust in summer—above town. Or, if you just waited another half hour, another round's worth, it would come walking through those barroom doors on Friday night.

It was time, is what it was. Mountain Time is a peculiar phenomenon, combining the poignancy of awesome length and fleeting brevity; and in Telluride in those days you got it full-on and unadorned. There were those autumns that absolutely embodied what the Japanese call *aware*—beauty made more intense by the anguish of its too quick passing. You wanted to grab those dusks when the air was thick with flying aspen leaves and that crabapple scent of fallen leaves consumed by the black forest floor, take them and somehow save them for yourself forever.

You hiked up the Wasatch Trail in mists and drizzles through drifting shrouds of cloud with someone you'd just met (she was just visiting, was leaving the next day), cold and wild, and on the way back down Bridal Veil, knees aching and chilled, you crazily felt you had fallen in love with her, even though (or perhaps because) you knew you would never see each other again. The thunder rumbled on the hidden peaks, and you stopped at the base of Bridal Veil, in the crystalline nimbus of the freezing spray, in the deafening white-noise silence of shattering water, and kissed.

Of course, you never saw her again. And during the lonesome winter that followed, you burned the memories to try and stay warm. But the winters went on so long, so damned long.

Law and Order,
San Juan–Style

S ome things never really change, it seems: like law and order, crime and punishment, sin and retribution.

Almost every local knows, and visitors soon find out,
that Butch Cassidy and the Sundance Kid robbed their first
bank, the First National, here in Telluride, in 1889, getting away
with $24,000 in funds meant for the miners' upcoming payday.
But Butch and Sundance were outsiders, just passing through;
the real interesting stuff is the homegrown badness, the local
(and, alas, rich) tradition of misdemeanor, felony, and crimes
against God and Nature. "To hell you ride," the train conductors

used to tell Telluride-bound train passengers back in the old mining days, and they weren't exaggerating. This little burg has produced way more than its share of wrongdoing and wildness since its very beginning.

The other day, I went through the county sheriff's file of prisoners booked into the local jail, 1917 through 1926. A character named E. G. Wilson, nationality *"American,"* male, twenty-two, was arrested for *"Dope"* and *"found out to be all Right and was turned loose"* after costing the county two dollars for four meals. His cohort, twenty-six-year-old *"Mrs. Massey,"* also *"American,"* was described as having *"all the Dope needdles & things found on her but no dope so she was Released."*

A Mrs. H. Lynde was arrested as a *"Habitual User of Morphine."* George Shoolas, nationality *"Greek,"* was booked for being a *"foren born non citisen with firearms"* and was *"fined $25 and costs of $14.45 and Released . . ."*

An *"Austrian"* named John Dermedi was fined $225 for *"Bootlegging."* Fred Rockwell, American, was sentenced to ninety days in county jail for *"Shooting H. M. Hummell at Placerville in head."*

Mrs. Ebel Gregory was arrested for *"Insanity"* by Sheriff Rico but was *"found to be normal and Was Released."*

A *"Sweede"* with the unlikely Scandinavian name of W. H. Billings was arrested for *"shooting Gus Ruff"* but was *"Released"* for *"insufficient evidence."*

A *"PiUte, Indian"* named *"Mormon Joe, also known as Wechena,"* age *"50 or over,"* was arrested for murder.

During World War I, there were many, many *"Slackers"* (draft dodgers), and at least one *"Treason"* (R. O. Grimm, *"American"*).

"4 Indians, Jim Curley, Jaun Hoskeneshenbega, Hosken Nezbqa, Hoshen Janbega," were arrested for *"Killing Deer in Lower West End of Co., fined $100.00 and costs. Each Fine Suspended on behalf thay do not come back to Colo. for the Purpose of hunting Deer or game out of season . . . thence shiped to Shiprock."*

T. D. Smith shot Carl Blakaley after Blakaley beat him up; Smith was released on $1,000 bond, while Blakaley *"surved 30 days in County Jail."*

An *"Aemirican"* (with a backwards *n*) John Davies was arrested for *"Vage and Begging Resdince of City and Citzens"*—*"Had Herring in Sherriff office an* [backwards *n* again] *Turned Loose if He Wood Leave City And County."*

The line between criminal and hero seems to blur, in the mountains. We should never forget, ever, that Telluride survives today only because of a felony committed eighty years ago, by a man now nearly forgotten in Telluride.

The year was 1929: the Great Depression. A small, diffident milquetoast with the heart of a lion named Charles Delos "Buck" Waggoner was president of the Bank of Telluride.

Knowing that the B of T, which contained the savings of nearly every poor miner, merchant, and wrangler in town, was about to go bust, Waggoner went up to Denver and borrowed a total of $500,000 from six of the largest banks in New York through six big Denver banks, with the aid of some strategic, um, tall tale wagging. He then went to New York City, picked up the proceeds of his trickery, covered the Bank of Telluride's debits, making it solvent again, and then disappeared, only to be apprehended in

Newcastle, Wyoming. He had just $400 in his wallet when caught. After a trial in New York he served three years in prison and emerged at age fifty-six a ruined man, forgotten in the town he had saved. A series of unlucky breaks brought him finally to Reno, Nevada, where he went blind and died, alone.

The Bank of Telluride went under in 1934, not to re-open till the mid-1960s. Still, C. D. Waggoner is our True Hero, a Revolutionary Bandit in pince-nez and suspenders, a Kwazy Wabbit Che standing atop the barricades calling out, "No passaran—please?" Forget the posers and punks like Butch and Sundance. We should build a statue to Buck Waggoner, right in front of the county courthouse, across from the Elks Club, where we can look upon it every day and think, Now, there's a real Mountain Man! A banker who robbed banks to try and save his own town.

Are things any less wild today? Well, not really.

One of our most recent renowned police cases involved a drug raid on a ranch house out in the West End. Sheriff's deputies discovered, among other things, an inflatable sex doll, along with hundreds of Polaroids of local cowpokes and cowgals in various coital combinations with the dummy.

Another raid in the same area was triggered when lawmen discovered that the tires on exhibit in front of a local gas station were missing. Black smoke rising from the fields outside town led them to a bonfire of burning tires in front of a certain homestead, a bunch of rural rowdies, and a litany of crimes including larceny (the tires), underage drinking, underage sex, hunting out of season, and drunk and disorderly conduct. It was not the first mass bust at the homestead. Said one bemused officer, "As soon as we see the tires missing in front of McSorley's, we head right for the Hoonslaw Farm and arrest everybody we see. Those fools always steal tires from the same place, take 'em home, build a bonfire, get drunk, and then go crazy. It makes our job pretty easy. Ya think they'd learn."

Justice is still swift out here, too. When a certain unpopular Telluride town marshal, fond of boasting of his "quick draw," shot Don Darvon's dog back in the seventies, Darvon snuck up on the marshal's house, waited till the crapulous lawman stripped and got into the bathtub, and then kicked in the front door, stormed into the bathroom, dragged the marshal out of the tub, and beat the bejayzus out of him. Darvon won the acclaim of the entire community.

On the opposite side of the thin blue line, our county sheriff for the last many years has been an outspoken libertarian and Dudley Do-Right lookalike by the name of Bill Masters. Sheriff Bill has his own style, no doubt about it.

For instance: A particularly unsavory, whiny character was sentenced to serve six months or so in Bill's county jail down in Ilium Valley, a mile below my house. This fellow was a New Agey, trendy kind of criminal, with all the usual excuses gleaned from pop psychology and situation ethics. He introduced himself to Bill by saying, "You know, I was abused when I was a kid. That's how I turned out wrong."

"Well, now you're in my jail, and you're gonna get abused some more," Bill replied unsympathetically.

When a big-time dope dealer was arrested in one of Telluride's expensive outlying neighborhoods, Bill tried to keep the government from confiscating the man's house and selling it. Wasn't right, he said. It violated the man's rights. And when the government went ahead and did it anyhow, and turned over a cut of the take to the San Miguel County Sheriff's Department to buy more guns, radios, and such, Bill argued (unsuccessfully) to use the money for a free walk-in drug treatment facility in Telluride instead.

One time, Masters, some of his deputies, and lawmen from adjoining counties went out to the West End, to a shack in a canyon in the arid, oxidized uranium country, to arrest a much wanted felon. They found the shack deserted but sensed that the felon was watching them from the cliffs above.

They waited, and waited, and waited some more. It was a hot day. The lawmen called out over their bullhorns again and again, ordering the man to surrender himself. No reply. More waiting, as the sun inched its way with maddening slowness across the bald blue sky.

Finally, as sundown approached, Sheriff Bill had had enough. He turned to one of the other lawmen, who knew the bad man well. "Tell me something. Is he the kind of guy who'd shoot a cop?"

The other man considered a moment or two. "Nah, he don't have the balls."

Sheriff Bill seized the bullhorn. "KARSEY," he bellowed. "I'M GIVIN' YOU FIVE MINUTES TO SURRENDER, OR I'M BURNIN' YOUR DAMNED HOUSE DOWN."

No reply from the invisible watcher in the cliffs.

Bill studied his watch. When precisely five minutes were gone, he went into the shack, soaked some rags in kerosene, heaped them on the floor, and then tossed a lit match on the pile. Flames erupted to the ceiling.

Bill walked outside and grabbed the bullhorn again. He faced the cliffs. "DON'T SAY I DIDN'T WARN YUH," he yelled. Still no reply.

The dry wood shack was already a flaming pyre, floor to roof. A couple of the other cops were smiling, despite themselves. Somebody chuckled. The chuckling spread, and turned to laughter. "Wisht I'd brung a camera," somebody said.

"Well, that's that," Bill said to the rest of the posse. They got in their cars and 4WDs, started up their engines, and one by one they drove back out the dusty dirt road toward the highway, miles away. As the last vehicle disappeared toward home, the outlaw's hideout collapsed in on itself.

As Bill told me later, "The guy didn't have a place to live anymore, so he pulled up stakes and left the county. We never saw him again. Case closed."

Disappointment
Valley

S ometime in the 1880s, in the summer, a band of Ute Indians left their reservation near Mesa Verde to hunt deer on
their tribe's ancestral lands around the headwaters of Little
Beaver Creek, near Disappointment Valley. The hunting party
consisted of half a dozen to a dozen men ("bucks," in the racist
parlance of the day) and two "squaws," the younger a fifteen-
year-old girl, the older a mother with her baby.

According to the local cattlemen, the Indians' "chief," Osipah,
had sent a threatening message to them: "Tell the cowmen we
are coming on their range and would [sic] fight to kill." How the
supposed message was sent, and to whom, is unclear. The cow-

boy sources go on to say that the Utes were slaughtering hundreds of "big buck deer" every year in the Disappointment Valley, taking the hides and then burning all the precious meat in bonfires, and the cattlemen wanted to stop them. Other Anglo sources accused the Utes of rustling and killing the ranchers' cattle, while some said Osipah's party was part of an invading Ute army bent on attacking all the white settlements in the area, annihilating men, women, and children.

All of the above sound like excuses manufactured after the fact, especially given the facts of the "battle" itself. The most likely reasons behind the attack: the Utes occasionally rustled cattle from the local ranchers, Osipah's band possessed a valuable herd of horses the whites wanted, and, more than anything, the overwhelming climate of racism that pervaded Cowboy Culture in the nineteenth century. Westerners back then openly despised Mexicans, blacks, and Indians as subhumans.

The Beaver Creek Massacre of Osipah's band in Disappointment Valley happened something like this. A dozen or more Lone Cone and Disappointment Valley cowboys, all "respectable citizens" and ancestors of today's local ranching families, took time off from their ranching, formed an armed posse, and crept up on the peaceful encampment of Utes, Osipah and his extended family, before dawn. The Utes had no lookouts or pickets out; they obviously had no expectation of danger.

The cowboys took up positions on a ridge overlooking the camp. As soon as the camp began to stir, they opened fire. After less than a minute, Osipah and his "bucks" and the fifteen-year-old "squaw" lay dead. When the older woman suddenly broke from one of the tepees with her baby in her arms and fled down Beaver Creek, the cowboys took careful aim and gunned her down. Somehow she got to her feet and continued her flight. Another cowboy shot her, and again she fell, only to get up once more and keep running. When a third shot failed to stop her, a cowboy named Jim Nash supposedly stopped the others from shooting with the words, "Let her go—she can't get far."

The brave cowboys then rounded up the Utes' valuable herd of horses, from 50 to 150 animals, and took them as "spoils of war." They left the dead Indians lying on the ground. That same day, two other local cowboys ambushed and killed a solitary Ute horseman riding across Lone Mesa, cut his head off, and threw the dismembered body over a cliff. One of the men returned home with the head in a sack, as a trophy.

According to Ute stories, the woman who fled actually survived her wounds. But her baby died, smothered by her mother by accident as the woman tried to stop her from crying, fearing the cowboys were trying to track them down. Cowboy and Indian sources agree in their description of the woman. She had a unique diamond-shaped birthmark on her face: "the diamond-faced squaw."

Backtrailing or cutting track to the truth of this story, we find we are not as innocent as we thought, or hoped. One wonders if that last severed head lies, mummified, in some trunk in a ranch attic out in the West End.

But hell, our predecessors here in San Miguel County were just as bad to each other. Telluride, as mentioned earlier, is where the

International Workers of the World's mine union was busted back at the beginning of the century. Leading the mine owners and their hired goons was a shit-heel Ivy League smoothie named Bulkeley Wells who came west with someone else's money, à la George W. Bush, if you will, to make a fortune. Striking miners were beaten, murdered, and hauled by train with their families in midwinter and dumped on top of Dallas Divide. The old stone fort high atop Imogene Pass, on the back Jeep road between Telluride and Ouray, was built not to fight the poor Utes, but to guard against union miners sneaking back to Telluride to retrieve their possessions or try and find work.

Of course, today's Telluride hustlers, real estate parvenus, and graspies idolize Wells, as well they might. How much has really changed in these parts? Twenty-odd years ago, during some summer festival or other down in Durango, "cowboys" killed a young Ute man in a fight and then dragged his corpse through town behind their pickup. And then there was the redneck high school gang down in Farmington about the same time who tortured skid row Navajos to death for fun, were finally arrested, and got off with a slap on the wrist from a local judge. But in their case, the local Navajo holy men got together and put a kind of hex on them, and the three guilty youths ended up suffering extremely horrible fates ex judicio. Hexes do exist: there are people who can tweak, focus, and intensify karma, consequences.

Speaking of hexes, there is supposed to be a Ute curse on the Telluride Valley.

According to the story, the Utes used to summer in the valley, living off riches of deer, elk, bighorn sheep, berries and sweet tubers and roots. The valley was sacred to the Raccoon, who, along with Coyote, makes up the Trickster Tag Team of Native America. You could hunt anything else in the valley, but not raccoons.

One day, a foolish young boy was out hunting with his new bow and arrow when he spied a huge, beautiful raccoon sunning himself in a forest glade. He remembered the prohibition, but he coveted the thick, plush fur. It would make a perfect hat for the long, icy winters down on the southern rivers. No one was around to see. He hesitated, then raised his bow, notched an arrow, and SPAAANNNGGG!! The arrow pierced the raccoon's breast, straight through the heart, impaling him.

But instead of dying, the Raccoon, for it was He, the eternal, omnipotent immanence behind the creature, pulled the arrow from his body, and spoke: "You and your people must leave my valley. You can never come here again. Anyone who ever tries to live here in the future will be unhappy."

The Utes broke camp and left the valley the next morning, never to return. The Eternal Raccoon was reincarnated as Coonskin Mountain, the big humped ridge that presides over the valley from the south; you can still see the demigod's tail in the form of the westerly ridge, striped with parallel stands of light-colored aspen and dark conifers.

Who knows the provenance and authenticity of the legend? The Americas, particularly the western United States, is full to bursting with apocryphal Indian Maidens, Lovelorn Warriors,

Tutelary Beavers, and Friendly Bears, immortalized in obscure locally published books by spinster poets and on cafe placemats. The story sounds, well, *funny*, like maybe it was written after the fact, to justify the miners' expulsion of the Utes from these, their native mountains. After all, if they were already gone, then it was nobody's fault they weren't still here.

And yet, as one old-timer once told me at the Elks Club at one in the morning, "Just because it never really happened doesn't mean it's not true."

The Black Book

There is another Telluride myth, this one from the mining era: the Legend of the Black Book.

Boom or bust, Telluride has always had a split personality. North of Main Street lived the "respectable" folks: East Coasters, British, Germans, Australians, the rich and ethnically favored who ran the place. Big, genteel houses, the flower of Victorian architecture, sat amid green lawns and elaborate gardens. This was a world of horse buggies and picnics, holiday tours of Europe, peripatetic lecturers at the Opera House, and two-foot by one-foot beefsteaks, lobster and possum, vichyssoise and fresh strawberries at the Sheridan's renowned restaurant.

South of Main teemed with the undesirables and outcasts. Boarding houses were crammed with tough Swedes, Finns, Cornishmen, and eastern Europeans, miners all, along with Chinese, half-breeds, and "niggers." In an average year during the Boom days, over a hundred prostitutes, many of them opium addicts, worked at dance halls and brothels like the Pick & Gad, Silver Bell, Gold Belt, Big Swede, and Idle Hour.

South of Main made its own rules. Loud music played far into the night. Gambling games, many of them rigged, went on incessantly. A miner would come down to Telluride after six solid months at one of the high tunnels like Rock of Ages or the Lewis, pockets stuffed with money. After a weekend south of Main, amid the good-time gals, the gaming tables, and the jugs of moonshine, he trudged back up the mountain, flat broke.

It was a cruel little Floating World. When prostitutes were in short supply, Telluride pimps would drug and kidnap innocent young women in the neighboring towns, take them back up to Telluride, and put them to work. Justice was bent backwards and made a mockery. One popular town marshal, Jim Clark, moonlighted as an armed robber to supplement his cop's pay. When the town tried to fire him, he refused to quit; shortly thereafter, he was shot and killed by a sniper firing from the roof of the San Juan Saloon. The shooter, of course, escaped.

The fine folks north of Main considered themselves far above all this vulgarity and violence, of course (though the town government wasn't too proud to tax each brothel owner $150 a week in "licensing fees").

Which brings us to the Black Book.

According to the stories, a certain old-timer, sickened by the sanctimony of his fellow citizens, compiled a detailed list of how the two halves of town "mingled" over the years. And my, how they mingled! According to another now deceased ancient who claimed to have actually seen the book, it catalogs which north-of-Main top hats married good-time girls from south of the line and sired families by them, after taking care to erase all record of the wives' pasts. Which pillars of the community had a yen for the silky smoke of yen shee gow and spent their nights behind the Chinese laundry kicking the gong around? Which bankrupt and busted boomer sold his own daughter to the Golden Belt or the Pick & Gad to raise capital for his next try, and then, when he hit the mother lode, decided he was too respectable to take her back into the family? Which church-going, Alleluja-braying pillar of the community owed his fortune to the "tragic accident," the cave-in that killed his partners and left the whole claim to him?

Those were heartless times. Hike up the Judd Wiebe Trail sometime from Coronet Creek. At the top of the switchbacks, you enter a dreamy summer glade where light in a dozen shades of green dances through the treetops and splashes and spatters on the dank ground. Eider Creek makes soft silver sounds in the shadows. Fallen trees melt like giant candles in the velvet gloom. You half expect to see Titania and White Buffalo Woman slow-dancing together cheek to cheek, bare feet ankle deep in wild-flowers.

The place is called Eppes Park. Back in the late nineteenth century, this enchanted spot was the site of Telluride's pesthouse.

When plagues swept the mining camps in the Upper Telluride Valley, the victims were hauled up to this spot above town and left, in a crude barnlike building, to die. No one dared tend to them, ease their suffering; nobody but a few prostitutes, young women with the courage of their own utter hopelessness and the instinct for mercy so often found in those who have asked their whole lives for mercy and received none.

A strange place, this Eppes Park. Imagine the agonies, the excruciating sense of abandonment, the screams in the night heard all the way down in town, south of Main ("Play LOUDER, fer God's sake, piano-man!"). And now, it looks and feels purely like Paradise. A paradise where once upon a time men created their own little piece of Hell.

Somewhere in Montrose, in a storage locker or a cardboard carton in someone's attic, is the Black Book. It's all in there: the truth that no one wants to know. And somewhere down on the Ute reservations, the elders know what really went down in the Disappointment Valley, way back when. The names and ages of the dead, just how they died, who the cowboys were and what they stole. And they also know this truth: that in our time, the Iron Age, only the innocent are punished. The guilty go free and prosper.

Cabin Fever

Not everyone makes it, now, then, or ever. In this country of slippery slopes and hidden drop-offs, disaster is never more than a half step away. And karma strikes fast in the thin air.

They came from California in the late seventies. Chuck, a fierce-eyed, skinny, guitar-pickin' grad school dropout, age thirty-two, and his girlfriend, Andrea, just twenty, five-foot-one of trouble, with the innocent face of an Aztec angel and the body of a fertility goddess on the rampage.

Andrea had a friend already there, Betsy, who was waitressing at the Senate, and who wrote her and said, "This is The Place." Chuck had just given up for the second and last time on his M.A. in history at San Luis Obispo, and Andrea, she didn't have that much to give up: she was riding her beauty on the paths of least resistance. In this case, it was Chuck.

Telluride at that time was a bad place to bring a pretty woman. There had always been too many men and not enough women there, it seemed. News of a new girl in town was greeted with the kind of excitement a new gold or silver strike would have evoked in the old days. That was the main reason Betsy had thrived there. Back in Northern California she had been just another blue-eyed blond with a slim boyish body, two years of junior college, and a fondness for partying—not poison, but not exactly Popular with a big, glowing *P* either. In T'ride, she had parlayed her way through at least a dozen guys in eighteen months and ended up with a free place to live courtesy of her coke-dealing attorney boyfriend, and a couple of steady, part-time, sneak-around dudes on the side. Another guy, an older, married realtor, wanted her to run off to Mexico with him in the spring.

Chuck and Andrea arrived late in the summer, driving Chuck's VW camper van, and quickly settled in courtesy of Betsy in an old mining cabin down in Fall Creek. Rent free, as it belonged to a wealthy client of Betsy's boyfriend, Alex, who lived in New York. Chuck got a job as a half-time paralegal in Alex's office, and Andrea started waitressing nights with Betsy at the Senate.

Back in San L.O. Chuck's relationship with Andrea had been balanced by his intelligence, his wit, his many friends. But up here in the mountains Andrea suddenly found she held all the aces with her youth, beauty, and air of sexual promise. Her first night at work a local mollusk named Louis Lazard, tall, potbellied, with loads of dank curly hair and a heavy Navajo squash-blossom necklace, saw her from the bar, decided on the spot to have dinner, made sure he sat at one of her tables, and then, after he ate, ordered two glasses of Grand Marnier and asked Andrea to drink one with him. Which she did. He left her a fifty-dollar tip with a half gram of coke folded up inside.

Chuck had worked late on Alex's law files and grabbed a late burger and a beer at the Roma before coming by to drive Andrea home. He was tired, and she was wired, from the tips and the admiration and the ease of her new job. They fought in the car on the way home, after he asked her why she looked so damned happy. She replied, Next time do me a favor and go home, and I'll stay in town. Back at the cabin she broke out the coke, and they had great, grinding, makeup sex. Chuck exulted, but while Andrea howled on all fours like a wolf at the full moon out the window, she was thinking about Louis Lazard and the way he had looked at her and spoken to her, sly and insinuating.

By the time summer slid into autumn Andrea was running around with Louis on the side and had also tumbled into bed once with Alex. Chuck never really found out, partly because he didn't want to; it was easier to pretend.

At the town Halloween Party in the old Quonset Hut, things came to a head. Chuck and Andrea had taken 'shrooms and came dressed as a riverboat gambler and a dance hall girl, respectively. It was a haunted night, clouds racing over the moon, the air full of the sweet smell of rotting leaves, the peaks glowing with new snow, an anguished kind of beauty. Andrea drank too much on top of the psilocybin and disappeared into the night with Louis. Chuck went crazy and ran out into the night. He went looking for her at Alex's, not knowing where else to go. Betsy was there alone, after a fight with Alex, who had taken off for Aspen with someone else.

Chuck and Betsy had never liked each other. Chuck blamed Betsy for Andrea's straying, while she had always felt threatened by Chuck's vaguely supercilious air of intelligence. But this night she was angry at Alex, and hurt, plus she had put away a half bottle of Alex's scotch to numb her sorrows. And Chuck, for his part, was stoned out of his mind and gnawed with jealousy and lovesickness. Betsy ended up going back to the cabin with Chuck and spent the night in bed with him after a perfunctory bout of because-it's-there lovemaking.

They were drinking coffee together on the front steps the next morning, Betsy in nothing but a ski sweater (one of Andrea's), Chuck in a T-shirt and jockey shorts, when Louis Lazard pulled up in his BMW with Andrea next to him, screeching to a stop in a roostertail of dust. Lazard looked furious; Andrea looked like a demented ghost, hollow eyed and pale.

She leapt from the car, kicked the door shut behind her, and as Louis peeled away giving everyone the middle finger, she rushed to Chuck and flung herself in his arms. Despite himself, he embraced her tenderly. After she had left the Quonset the night before with Louis, they ended up at another party, at the Ski Ranches, where she had begun dancing with some guy she had never met. "I was just having fun," she whimpered to Chuck; Betsy smiled with a hint of bitterness in the background. She fought with the jealous Louis; he dragged her back to his place, whereupon she threw up all over his black satin sheets, his Persian antique carpet, his black cat, Satan, and his $2,000 Swedish turntable. Now he hated her, and she hated him.

Somehow, it seemed, things had evened up.

Winter is a time when things seize up, freeze up, muffled by the snow, the darkness, the cold. Chuck spent $650 he couldn't afford on an old Subaru 4WD station wagon for Andrea so she could commute without hassle. He got a new job on the ski mountain doing lift maintenance, and Andrea kept working at the Senate.

An illusion of peace settled over their relationship. It was a five-minute ski back in to their cabin, up the switchbacked driveway, and sometimes on the long nights when a big norther dumped flakes the size of postage stamps outside, Chuck imagined this life going on . . . not forever, of course, but as long as they lived.

The propane heater roared softly, and Chuck read—Proust, Dostoevsky, Gogol—while Andrea knitted or painted watercolors or nursed one of her gigantic organic soups or stews on the stove. Life seemed good, and Chuck, without really noticing it, was falling deeper and more inextricably in love with Andrea. And he mistook her seeming tranquillity for contentment, her feline nestling for affection. What it was, was winter, of course: a Winter Thing, simple biology, warmth and shelter, like hibernation. But Chuck didn't know that.

As the winter began to slowly thaw, Chuck dreamed grand dreams of going to Mexico with Andrea, and then, yep, asking her to marry him. She went along with the Mexico part; he didn't tell her about the marrying scheme. They looked at maps and guidebooks, of Baja, Yucatán, Nayarit: palm trees swaying, surf rolling in, palapas in the glittering sun. He laughed and talked, on and on, about how great it was going to be. She smiled, a Gioconda smile that could have meant anything.

And it might have worked out—the Mexico part, anyway—except for . . . well, except for the mountains. Two days before the ski area closed, a week before they were going to drive south, Chuck caught an edge skiing down from work and got a nasty greenstick of the left fibula. He ended up with a huge cast and a refillable prescription for Percocet and Tylenol 3, courtesy of the kindly old town doc.

As the ski area closed and everyone they knew fled for beaches or fishing jobs in Alaska or the canyons of Utah, Chuck and Andrea found themselves marooned in a typical Rocky Mountain winter's end: insane wet snows, droning winds, mud, the aspens still bare as bones. Even if you're happy, that season can make you sad.

At first Andrea was sympathetic to Chuck: he was really stuck, couldn't drive with his leg; she had to take him everywhere (not that there was anywhere to go). But after a while (make it two weeks and change), it was wearing thin. Especially, as Chuck was one of those people who react negatively to opiates. The meds made him, variously, groggy, ill tempered, bathetic, depressed, childishly needy. And Andrea had to deal with it all. It sucks, she said to herself, over and over. Here she was, still twenty for two more months and painfully ripe, in the springtime goddammit, and she was stuck in a frozen wind tunnel with

Cabin Fever

a Grumpy Old Man. The stormy days were the worst, when the wind howled as if in misery or commiseration over the mud and the frozen crust, thrashing the trees, hurling grapnel or sleet. And almost all the days were stormy.

On one of those days, after forty-eight hours of the same and a week without a glimpse of the sun, after Chuck had inflicted a particularly obnoxious twenty-four hours on her, throwing things, yelling at her, then crying, then burning himself deliberately with a match, Andrea decided to do something. While Chuck dozed off, she hurriedly packed a few things in the Subaru he had bought her and left a note: "Gone to town to buy food & check mail—luv Andrea."

When she drove away, she thought, I'll never see him or that damned fucking cabin again. She felt a tinge of sadness for Chuck, but it was consumed by this huge wave of ecstatic relief, a weightless careless joy beyond compare, that swept over her.

When Chuck came to, it was already dark out again. The cabin was shuddering in the wind, creaking and banging. There were no lights on, and it was terribly cold. He called out for Andrea, but no answer came.

He managed to get to his feet, find matches, and light one of the kerosene lamps. He found Andrea's note on the table, crumpled it angrily, and threw it across the room. When he tried to turn the heater up, nothing happened. He got a flashlight and gimped outside to the propane tank. It had chosen this exact accursed day to run dry. Paranoid notions raced through his brain: Aha! Plans are being made without me. They think they can get me, but they don't know Chuck Fasched, do they?

Inside again, he got out a Percocet and two Tylenol 3s and washed them down with cold bitter coffee from the morning pot. He put on a sweater and his heavy down parka, but he was still shivering, freezing. He got the bottle of Crown Royal from under the sink and drank off two inches in a gulp, napalm down his gullet.

He sat at the kitchen table, drinking another inch of the Crown every twenty minutes. Waiting for Andrea. She would be back soon (he hadn't noticed her missing things). The goddamn bitch. Beautiful Andrea. His bride-to-be (he would ask her tonight). The whore . . . and where was she? He counted his remaining pills again and again: two and a half Percocets, eleven TC3s. He remembered that Andrea had an ancient Valium, a blue one, 10 mg, in an old bottle in the bathroom. He got that and took it.

When he came to this time, he was lying on the hard wooden floor, his cheek in an icy pool of his own saliva. His head throbbed, his leg ached: he must have hit it when he fell. There was no sign of Andrea, and the clock said 2:11. And the wind kept blowing outside like there was no tomorrow.

He turned on the radio. Nothing but static. KOTO was off the air.

That's when he got the brilliant idea of killing himself. Not really killing himself (one part of him whispered) but nearly killing himself, to be found in the nick of time by Andrea, who would then see just how much he loved her, just how wild about her he was. And then they would get married and live happily ever after. Or something, right?

Cabin Fever

He made a heap of all his remaining pills on the table, added a big bottle of aspirin, three or four Flexirils from who knows where, and started swallowing them, choking them down with the rest of the Crown.

By three A.M. the pills and the whiskey were gone, and he was still alive. So sick he could barely think or move coherently, but alive. He made a half-hearted attempt to cut his wrists with Andrea's leg razor, but that was tough because of the plastic guard on the blade. Still, he managed to make a dramatic-looking mess of both forearms before passing out again.

That's how Louis Lazard of all people (sent by Andrea to check on him) found him the next dawn: a hypothermic, semi-comatose mummy with a ghoul's face and wrists black with dried blood, lying on the floor of the cabin. The poor letch screamed and nearly fainted when he saw him, and then recovered enough to lug him out to his BMW and drive him at 75 miles an hour to the hospital in Montrose.

Chuck was released from the hospital a week later. But already up in Telluride his story had spread among the few locals there for off-season and was greeted, alas, with laughter. Committing suicide over a chick was bad enough, but failing at it. . . . He didn't know it, but he had earned a nickname that would last him a lifetime: "Not-Quite-Dead" Fasched, or more elaborately, "Fucked-Up" Chuck "Not-Quite-Dead" Fasched.

He was never quite the same after that: a few screws were knocked loose, permanently. He had a perpetual buzzing and ringing in his ears, his sense of balance was awry, and there was something, something, noticeably different about his eyes, a muddy Fool look to them that made strangers look twice when they saw him in a mall, on the street, in an airport.

Even ten, fifteen, twenty years later, when Betsy and he were married and running a janitorial business together, when he had put on fifty pounds, had two kids, and taken up Christianity, the name stuck to him . . . and the laughter. But he and Betsy and Louis and Louis's Filipina wife, Boots, were best friends, and all four sang in the church choir together.

Andrea? She never did find out about Chuck's melodramatic gesture on her behalf. While Louis was saving Chuck's life, Andrea was ripping off LL's emergency stash—not much, but hey, a thousand dollars in hundreds and a few grams of bad coke—and heading for Mexico. On a beach at San Blas she met a guy from California, Red, whom she'd known in high school. When the money and the time ran out, she drove north with him to Tahoe, where he got her a job dealing the tables. Blackjack, nothing hard. Two years later she married a seventy-year-old swinging millionaire dentist with a fifty-five-thousand-acre ranch, six exes, and a cocaine habit she happily shared. She never went back to the mountains.

Mountain Women

August 7, 1926, twenty-six year old Clara Dolan was arrested for
Assault With Intent to Kill & Murder. Broke out of jail
night Aug. 8 cutting locks on the doors and got away.
—San Miguel sheriff's jail log

Yep, Paradise could be a tough proposition, and the women there, well, they were even tougher.

I was having a bum spring, to say the least. I'd lost my two jobs, one as contributing editor to a climbing magazine, the other shoveling snow off hotel and condominium roofs before they caved in. The two jobs had brought in a sum total of about four hundred dollars a month. Not a whole hell of a lot. Still, four hundred was better than no hundred, which was what I was earning now.

71

My "savings" were just about depleted. I was down to two bulk jars apiece of Western Family peanut butter and jelly, twenty-seven dollars in my checking account, and a coffee can full of pennies with a few nickels and dimes mixed in. Twice a week I bought a loaf of half-priced day-old bread from B.I.T. I scraped the mold off and made stacks of PB&Js, washing them down with cheap black tea. I had long since flogged my skis, boots, poles, ice ax, and climbing rope at usurious late-season prices.

My latest serious lover, a sous chef at the Silverglade, had tossed me out of her life a few weeks ago: a triple disaster, because she took with her her car, which actually ran and which I'd been using, and her house, in which I was living. Leaving me with my barely mobile VW squareback, with its expired plates and tires as bald as a frog's ass. Not that I blamed her: I was a pretty grim specimen, when all was said and done. I had no plans for the future beyond hoping to write a best-seller or marry a rich woman, and one seemed less likely than the other.

The VW served one important purpose. It may not have been going anywhere fast, but it provided a roof over my head. I had the back seat folded down, forming a cramped sleeping area; the front seats were a mare's nest of books, plastic water bottles, food, dirty clothes, laundry soap, tapes, and a camp stove I used to make coffee. Efficiency apartment? This a deficiency non-apartment. My street address was a friend's snowed-up backyard on an alley, where I parked the car beyond the punitive grasp of the town marshals. Said friend also let me use his downstairs bathroom and his kitchen, but I tried not to. I didn't want to burn down the farm, at least till the snows melted.

These were the trials and vicissitudes of the modern Mountain Man.

To make things worse, it had been storming for eleven days straight: a bone-chilling spring blizzard, skies dark as dusk and days so short they were like bloody parentheses between the endless, dreary nights (N-I-G-H-T) (N-I-G-H-T) (N-I-G-H-T), and on and on, unto eternity. Typical March weather. The ski season still had nearly a month to go before closing, but it felt like it was already over. Everything did.

Salvation came, as it usually did back then, in the guise of a woman.

This was about the time I gave up drinking for good but hadn't quite yet. I had developed the habit of hanging out in various bars, the Sheridan, the Dollar, the Fly Me to the Moon, et al. I would sit there in the late afternoon into the evening, nursing a succession of Crown Royals, reading a book, writing in my notebook, talking with friends, maybe shooting a game or two of pool. Since I didn't have a house, the bars functioned as my living room–cum–office: a comfortable place to Be. It beat hunching like a hermit crab in the car, soggy and claustrophobic.

One rainy afternoon I was at the Moon, trying to read the latest by one of America's most popular authors. "The MK-88's heat sensors locked onto the thermal signature of Lopez's speeding Mercedes-Benz. In the nose cone, the warhead, ten pounds of plastic explosive wired to a Grey Lynx modular fuel-air component, armed itself. The spoiler fins steered the deadly package inexorably toward its target. . . ." If I could write like this, I thought, I wouldn't be living in a fucking car that doesn't run. *Merde:* it was hopeless.

The Golden Age is hard to recognize while it's in progress. Broke, snowed-in, cold, with no visible prospects, I couldn't help feeling sorry for myself. In fact, I rather enjoyed it. It must have been the German in me, The Sorrows of Young Werther and all that. . . . Someday I would look back in time and feel an almost insupportable longing for these bleak yet incandescent days and nights: the loneliness, the desperation, the folie grandeur.

Suddenly, a plume of beer hit my book from above, rebounding up in my face. "Dammit!" I slammed the book shut and started to get up, ready to hit somebody.

A redneck gal was standing there, grinning maliciously. Red hair, blue eyes, in Levis and a T-shirt that said, ONCE YOU TOSS YOUR HAT IN THE RING, YOU BETTER COWBOY UP. She held a Coors bottle upside down and continued to pour. Pure Scotch-Irish, the kind that should have a skull-and-crossbones warning label.

"What the hell—" I said.

"What the hell," she interrupted.

"—do you think you're doing?"

She finished pouring, turned, and hurled the empty bottle across the barroom into the trash barrel. SMASH!

"HEY!" The bartender yelled angrily.

"Hey, your fucking self," she replied. She slid in next to me. Took my half-empty shot of Crown Royal and tossed it down before I could stop her. Then grabbed the book and opened it at random. Read a few lines, and then tossed it dismissively back on the table. "Bombs away on the fucking bastards! Buy me a drink," she said.

"Why should I?"

"Because if you do you might just get lucky tonight."

"My dream come true," I said sarcastically.

"Pardner, you have no idea." She yelled over to the bartender. "Two Crowns." She looked at me. "Well?"

"Well, what?"

She rubbed the thumb and fingers of her right hand together.

I had no money, but I had a tab. I sighed in resignation. "They're on me," I called to the bartender.

She raised her eyebrows. "Tab, huh? You're looking better and better." She got up and went to get the drinks.

The bartender had finished pouring the two Crowns. She gave the drinks the fisheye. "You want to top those off, babe? And pour two more while you're at it," she told the bartender, Louise, who gave her a look of pure hatred as she got out two more glasses.

There was a band that night, the Flaming Creatures from Boulder. Lee danced like great electrical shocks were coursing through her body, starting out in her head and running south through her boyish torso, her flat belly, her narrow hips, down her skinny legs and out her cowboy boots into the floor. She drew a crowd, naturally, of whooping, leering guys, to which her response was, "What the fuckin' shit are you looking at?!?" When one diehard bought her a drink and handed it to her, she threw it in his face. She was a pistol.

That night in my car was like the Kama Sutra in a frozen phone booth. The next morning, she asked me if I wanted a job.

"Doing what?"

"Cleaning rooms at the Riverside."

"A maid?"

"Damn, you're smart. Yeah, a maid. Six an hour, plus anything you can steal."

I thought she was joking, but when I looked at her, I saw she wasn't.

I thought about it. "Who do I see?"

"Me. Congratulations, you just got the job."

Lee ran a crew of a half dozen women: two giantesses from Norwood, a Navajo girl who commuted four hours each day from the edge of the reservation and back, two Mexicans from Zacatecas, and a hippie from Ophir. The rhythm was straight out of the "Sorcerer's Apprentice," everything on the run till it was spotless. When we had a few minutes to spare, Lee would take food from the fridge in whatever unit we were cleaning and cook up a meal for the two of us, fried egg sandwiches, burgers, coffee. If there was booze, and there almost always was, she took that, too: a couple of beers, or a shot of whiskey, a glass of wine.

"Hey, check this out!" She was in the master bathroom going through the toiletries of the guests, a couple from New York.

"These people could open their own goddamn fucking hospital!"

She went through the prescription bottles, and there were a whole lot of them, taking what she wanted, till she had a half dozen Valiums, six Empirin with codeine, and four Percocets. "I don't know what these people have wrong with them, but whatever it is I hope I catch it!"

And then, "Hey!" Fifteen-mg Dexedrines. There were thirty-two of them; Lee took six.

"Aren't you afraid of getting caught?"

"Jesus, don't be such a motherfucking wuss. You're making me sorry we ever met."

She took two of the Dexedrines and washed them down with a handful of water. "Fasten your seatbelt, darlin', it's gonna be a long night tonight."

"Yeah?"

"Yeah. Speed makes me horny."

"Sorry about the windshield," Lee said the next morning. She'd kicked it into smithereens sometime around five in the morning, and now it was snowing in on our naked bodies. I didn't care. I don't know if I was in love or not, but I was deliriously, ass-over-teakettle something.

From then on, whenever Lee did something outrageous, which was only about a dozen times a day, that became her stock phrase: "Sorry about the windshield." When I asked her why we always ended up in my car instead of at her place, she said, "Can't. You know the Greek?"

He was the nervous-looking, paunchy, fifty-something, married-with-children manager of the Riverside.

"I'm living in his extra unit, rent free. The sonofabitch's in love with me," she snorted contemptuously.

"Isn't he mad? About us, I mean?"

"He doesn't know whether to piss up a rope or go blind. But he's also so fucking afraid his wife is gonna find out about me he doesn't dare say a fucking word."

Life with Lee, I was beginning to realize, was not a sustainable thing. Still, when she went back to Wyoming a week after the ski area closed, one step ahead of the law, it turned out, I missed her. A lot. Lee French Mitchell. And missing her, I decided, was a whole lot better than never having known her.

By midsummer I had sold a couple of stories to a slick outdoor magazine and gotten on, for $75 a week, at the latest incarnation of the Telluride weekly newspaper. Enough income to repair the VW and move into a room in a big old house up on the north side of town, for $150 a month.

My housemates were living proof that the mountains collect oddballs. "Freebie," who inhabited the shed on the alley, was a lanky, smelly, hairy vegan with insane eyes who managed the organic food co-op in town. Then there was stubby, monosyllabic Matt Carlson, who didn't do anything at all; rumor said he was a Disney heir, or in the witness protection program, or a federal fugitive. He spent twenty-three hours a day in his basement room, listening to his literally thousands of Grateful Dead tapes on an enormous floor-to-ceiling tape machine. (Five years later, he would die in Bolivia in a crashed DC-3 full of cocaine.)

An obnoxious young couple, Steve Castle and Summer Stevenson, friends of the house's dread absentee owner, fortyish Aspen divorcee Jools Pepperman, ruled the house from the first floor. Castle was one of those Ivy League dweebs who thinks the day he got his diploma from Yale, God reached down and touched him, saying, "Yea verily, you are now smarter and better than anyone else on the planet." He owned the newspaper I worked for, and Summer sold ads for the paper while nursing political ambitions and cultivating a wholly unjustified air of hauteur. "She looks like a goddam moose farted in her face," as Milo Muller put it succinctly.

I shared the second floor with Muller, a professional mountain bike racer built like a stiletto who, like me, hated everyone else in the house.

"Road rash," "bitchin' new derailleur," "alloy fatigue," "team weenie," "I Skylabbed," "rode so fast I had me a case of jet lag," "I freakin' assassinate their sorry ass": his was a simple, Martian world, from which the unhip and wheel-less were automatically barred. He kept about $150,000 dollars' worth of comp bikes chained and padlocked on the front porch, and mixed up arcane alchemical meals of juices, vitamins, yeast, North Atlantic fish liver oils, Jamaican molasses, and Great Ape growth hormones on his Cuisinart in the kitchen.

The house was hell on a semi-eligible bachelor like myself. Whenever I brought someone home, either the bad vibes of the Castle-Stevensons or Freebie's Precambrian BO (it wafted all the way from his odoriferous shack, permeating the whole house) or the seismic thud of the Dead, rising through the floorboards like Poe's telltale heart was sure to drive her away. I may as well have still been living in my car. That lucky bastard Muller had a girlfriend up in Aspen and spent most of his spare time up there when he wasn't on the race circuit.

Then, in July, things unexpectedly got better.

I had broken a tooth in a pickup soccer game one evening and went to the local dentist, Terry Brown, to get it ground down and capped. Lying in the dentist's chair on that rainy morning, the mask pumping nitrous oxide and oxygen up my nostrils, I had a revelation: that the town of Telluride outside the window had vanished, revealing the aboriginal valley with its skein of ponds, flooded meadows, and cold streams, with here and there great beaver lodges rearing up from the water like fortresses; herds of deer grazed in the timber, and an eagle guarded its aerie atop a dead lightning-struck pine where Timberline Hardware now does business, beneath the Masons Hall. Thunder growled up in the high basins, the ones we call Wasatch, Bridal Veil, La Junta, Marshall, but in reality have had no names for ten million years and still have no names, none that we would understand anyway. So it was, before the Utes came, before the White Man came, and so it will be again after we are gone, till the rivers all run dry and the mountains fall into the sea.

When I left, dazed and wobbly and with a throbbing jaw, I really believed that the building would vanish behind me, and there I would be, alone in the wilderness . . . the First (or Last) Man in the Valley.

No such luck, of course. The town was still there. So I went home and started recording the vision on my uncle's Second World War Olivetti, with a pot of Dragon's Well tea next to me to keep me going. The rain kept falling outside. When I was finished, I rolled the pages up in a zip-lock bag, stuck the bag in my daypack, put on an anorak and a baseball cap, and rode my rusty

Scott Teton down to the newspaper office. Avoiding Castle and Stevenson, I went into Mike Hitchcock's office, got out the story, and tossed it on his desk. Hitchcock looked up from a copy of *Guns & Ammo*.

"My column," I said.

"You're early. Is anything wrong?" I was famous, or infamous, for turning in my copy at the very last second.

"This one wrote itself."

"You're the William Butler Yeats of the San Juans now, huh? Should I make your next paycheck out to The Cosmos?" He started to scan the first page and read aloud: " 'I have discovered a Time Machine, and its name is Laughing Gas.'" He chuckled. " 'Like the tundra butterflies Nabokov hunted here back in the fifties, the delicate fluttering sky-blue fritillaries, we are the briefest of phenomena; in fact, the frailest .09-gram lepidoptera will outlive our concrete and steel, our trophy homes and bank balances. . . .' Well, in the case of *your* bank balance, that's probably true!"

I couldn't help but smile. Hitchcock, beer-swigging, unshaven hulk, descendant of one of Telluride's old hardrock mining families and one of the staunchest kingpins of the local Elks Club, was a joy to work with. He was famous for his practical jokes. When the Castle-Stevensons decreed that the only bathroom at the paper was reserved for them as "executives," that the rest of us peons would have to use the johns at the restaurant next door, Hitch sneaked in and stretched a sheet of Saran Wrap across the C-S's toilet. He then partially unscrewed the light bulb in the ceiling, emptied the soap dispenser and filled it with Krazy Glue, and sat back and waited.

Castle came bustling in at 8:30 A.M., after his usual hour of coffees with his sad-sack "important" friends. He went straight to the john, closed the door, turned on the light, cursed when no light appeared, unzipped, and let fly. His own urine rebounded at him, face to crotch, soaking his Brooks Brothers slacks and button-down shirt. More curses, these hysterical. And then, water running in the sink, and the squeak of the soap dispenser, followed by a banshee's wail when the soap turned out to be mucilage. Castle suspected Hitchcock was the guilty one but could never prove it. Anyway, he couldn't fire Hitch: Hitch was the only one there who knew how to run a newspaper.

He kept reading: "Blah blah blah—" Then he declaimed the conclusion dramatically: " 'Maybe it would have been better, in the long run, if none of us had ever been here: the hunters, the miners, the resort builders, the speculators and fun hogs. We've made a lot of noise, and cut things down and dug things up, and I'm not sure if it's really mattered at all. When everything's said and done, all we leave behind are our ghosts, as insubstantial as the shifting light in the aspen groves, the clouds burning up in the moon. . . .' "

He looked up at me. "I'm not sure what the hell it means—"

"Me neither."

"—but I like it."

The column ran in Friday's paper. That night I was leaving a particularly awful town council meeting, in which the council took three hours and change to back off from a controversial down-zoning of Lot 8 and appoint a Special Ad Hoc Committee to study the issue, trying to figure out the lead for my piece:

"On Friday night, the Telluride Town Council voted to defer judgment—table—avoid—"

I stepped out into the street when suddenly someone spoke my name. "Rob?"

I turned around.

The speaker was a young woman I had seen a couple of times before, a newcomer in town; her name was something strange and geographical—Nevada? Alaska? Athens? She was the color of soft dust, with black hair tangled and shining, and huge Sephardic eyes.

She held out her hand. "Shenandoah Goldsmith." We shook. A sheaf of cheap Indian glass bracelets jingled. She actually blushed and looked away. She was wearing some kind of hot, aching scent, like Wind Song and Tea Rose together.

"Listen, I really liked your column today—" She laughed. "I mean, that's so weak, 'liked'—it was amazing—"

There was a lump in my throat; I had trouble talking. "Well, thanks," I said lamely. Somehow we were walking together, as if by some unspoken understanding. And somehow we both began laughing, at ourselves and each other, us.

What was she wearing, anyhow? I had a vague impression of a man's white dress shirt carelessly half-unbuttoned, jeans worn to the softness of velvet, a brown calfskin jacket, and a silver heart-shaped locket on a thin tarnished chain resting between her breasts.

She was working for KOTO, as a news intern, and before she moved to Telluride two months earlier she'd been in Paris for a year, singing and modeling; and before that, India, a Rajneesh ashram in the foothills of the Himalayas, and before that a kibbutz in Israel, after she dropped out of Bennington. And, yes, Shenandoah was really her name, courtesy of her father, a radical (but somehow, through some highly questionable taxi medallion business, rich as hell) lawyer in New York with a thing for Native Americans; he used to beat a tom-tom at Passover and chant a Babelized brew of Hebrew and original poetry à la Gary Snyder about Coyote and Moses, Ruth and Pocahontas, Ezekiel and Crazy Horse.

Well, that was Telluride, all right. People came to the mountains the same way they ran away to join the circus or the Foreign Legion: to jettison the past and reinvent their future. And what better place? The drastic scale, altitude, isolation, all encouraged it. The very thinness of the air stoned you with every breath you took. You got only 45 percent of the oxygen you got at sea level; maybe that meant you told only 45 percent of the truth, to yourself and others. Leaving a realm not unreal so much as surreal, a waking dream.

Down in the flatlands lives were strictly nonfiction, documentary. Up here, high up, existence was unconstrained: magical realism was loosed upon the world. Seductive and dangerous in equal portions. The problem is, love in the mountains tends to be a fritillary affair: gorgeous, evanescent, more light than substance. Or, to borrow another Rocky analogy, mountain love is like a salted claim: you see all these bright, precious nuggets of gold lying around, and you think you've struck it rich, only to find that those nuggets are all there is, left there to trick the unwary. Beneath them is nothingness, dark useless nothing-ness. *Caveat emptor,* friend.

We kept walking, walking, talking and laughing together, and as we walked, the warmth of her body along with that venereal perfume she wore enveloped me. Down to the base of Bear Creek, around the Beaver Pond, up by the Pandora Mine; all the way up to the base of Bridal Veil Falls, where we kissed in the crystalline roar of the cataract. Back down through Lone Tree Cemetery into town, our arms around each other now, with another unspoken agreement somehow reached along the way: that we were to become lovers that night.

Too bad she waited two weeks, till after we were mired in a congee of passion, pain, and possessiveness, to tell me about the husband back east, who thought she was out there looking for a house for the two of them to buy; the husband and the two children, boy three, girl five, at home with husband and ancient Nana. Not to mention, till even later, the Serious Boyfriend, a clone of Rodin and Rodan, a great brute Hemingway of a sculptor with a studio down on Avenue A in Manhattan.

That one took the better part of two years to get out of alive (barely), two years during which I metamorphosed from outlaw lover to backdoor man to gibbering nimrod to craven cuckold and back again.

Well, what did I expect, falling in love 8,750 feet above sea level?

After Shenandoah, I ended up with Louise, the bartender who was serving drinks the night I met Lee. And after Louise, who left Telluride and me to study acupuncture in Hawaii, there was Tara, the Buddhist nun with the spectacular implants. I bummed *her* out so badly she retook her vows of celibacy when we broke up and is now, as far as I know, meditating in a cave outside Kathmandu, living on nettle soup. And after Tara, Scorpio Sally, who told me if I left her, she would kill me and then kill herself, and then had the nerve to leave *me*, not for another man but for another woman. And, more years and loves later, finally, Nancy, the woman I settled down with.

I discovered one thing, living and romancing in Telluride: mountain women are as dangerous as avalanches, but the ride's a lot more fun.

Sorry about the windshield.

Killers of the Dream

A couple of years ago, a hip rancher friend of mine sent me a packet of obscenely gory color photos she had somehow gotten her hands on. Taken by some sheepherders up north, around Meeker, the pix starred one Basillo C., Coyote Trapper Extraordinaire and World-Class Monster. See, Basillo didn't want to just kill coyotes, he wanted to do it with style. So he live-trapped the varmints, wired their jaws shut with barbed wire, and then let his dog pack tear them to pieces. And, of course, he had his little performance art tableaux immortalized on film. Understandable, yes? "Ah, the memories . . ."

Unfortunately for Mr. C., his sick pix fell into the hands of reporters from KCNC-TV in Denver, who proceeded to do a story on Basillo's animal torture operation. Basillo does his herding on

BLM (read our) lands, and the feds also got hold of the pictures and launched their own investigation.

Justice is served, right? Well, actually, wrong. The only penalty levied against the abhorrent Mr. C. was a $685 fine from the "government"; he didn't even lose his BLM grazing permit! Instead of being ostracized and shunned, he was lionized by locals and herders and ranchers from all over the state. Mr. C. remained totallly unrepentant.

"The only thing I did wrong was take pictures," he smirked to one interviewer.

The Colorado Rockies are full of this type, folks who just plain hate everything wild. It is a hatred that transcends reason. I remember talking to an old woman rancher from over by Ridgway a few years back. I mentioned that I had seen a badger on the prairies east of Boulder a few weeks before and how awesomely beautiful the animal had been, muscular and flat as a skillet, racing across the sun-scorched turf with that unique queer, undulating gait. "Unbelievably beautiful," I said.

The old woman squints at me from behind her scrim of cigarette smoke. "We found a big old badger in that field over there three, four years back." She looks happy, remembering. "Strong 'un. We had to lay a shovel across his neck with two grown men standing on either end, and even then it took him the better part of five minutes to die."

I don't know quite what to say—Congratulations? Bully for you? So I don't say anything.

A few years ago, the locals out in the West End of San Miguel County invented a new sport: slaughtering prairie dogs. They would drive out to the prairie dog village at day's end in their Jeeps, armed with "varmint guns" equipped with gigantic telescopic sights. Then they would hunker down and wait.

They never had to wait long.

Every time a prairie dog stuck its head out of the ground, someone would shoot it. BLAM! The tiny corpse, turned inside out and shredded by the heavy slug, pirouettes through the air in a puff of dust; it lands like a dirty rag dipped in blood, slapped down on the earth, and hard to believe it was something alive, quick, nerves aquiver, a split second ago.

BLAM! BLAM! BLAM! The little bodies pile up. The dusty field shivers and bends in the red heat. As the sun goes down, they collect the spent brass, to reload at home and use again, and pile into their Jeeps, hootin' and a-hollerin.' They leave the bodies of 317 prairie dogs there, to rot and stink.

A prairie dog village is one of North America's great natural wonders. The early western explorers described with awe colonies that stretched for miles across the shortgrass prairies, as far as the eye could see. Rare animals like the black-footed ferret and the burrowing owl share the subterranean burrows with the "dogs," along with more common associated species like *Crotalus horridis* (rattlesnakes), gophers, and foxes.

After a few years of shoot-and-let-rot "hunting," the colony in the San Miguel County's West End began to show unmistakable signs of damage. Many of the burrows were abandoned, empty. You could sit out there for a half hour to an hour some days and get off only a shot or two. It just wasn't fun anymore; in fact, it was kind of depressing. Members of the original group of shooters began to drift away; two weeks, three weeks, a whole month went by without anyone showing up to "pop a few 'dogs."

"Well, maybe it's a good thing," Fat Pat said one night at the bar. "This'll give the little bastards a chance ta re-populate. The way they breed, in a coupla more years there'll be twicet as many as there was before."

But it didn't work out that way; an invisible line had been crossed, impossible to tell exactly when, between survival and extinction, life and death. The prairie dogs just kept on dwindling away. Less than a year after Fat Pat's cheerful prediction, there weren't anymore. They were gone forever, which is a long, long time. Where there had been a bustling earthen hive, with thousands of watchful eyes and swift, sleek bodies, now there was nothing. Just an empty field, of scrub chaparral and dust, with an empty beer can glinting here and there.

Ever since anyone could remember, there had been a herd of elk up on the West Meadows of Turkey Creek Mesa. They mingled with Rowdy Roudebush's horses and kept grazing while human beings rode or walked among them. The old bull who led the herd was downright friendly. Local kids liked to take their out-of-town friends and cousins up to the Meadows. They'd stand by the fence in the evening and watch as the aged veteran ambled out of the forest and approached them across the glowing grass. He would stop short of the fence and stand there, regarding the children of Man philosophically, as if perhaps he knew his fate, while the Telluridian kids whispered, "That's our elk," their voices full of pride.

The people, like me, who moved to Telluride back in the seventies came for the mountains. The mountains, and to try to build lives to match them. Communards, poets, climbers, ski addicts, visionaries, the fact that we failed most of the time didn't diminish or detract from our original dreams. But the next big wave of émigrés, when Telluride began to become well known, "hot," were different. Oh, they talked the mountain talk all right: the splendor of the mountains, the uniqueness of the town, the wildness of the San Juan country. They talked, but they didn't walk the walk; in fact, most of them didn't look like they had ever walked anywhere. Real estate hustlers, "developers" ("Developers are to the Rockies as Serbs are to Kosovo"—barroom toilet graffito, Telluride, 1999), investors, ganefs of every rank, style, and persuasion.

One of these characters ended up in jail after selling national forest land to unwary visitors, claiming that he owned it! Others, still on the loose, specialized in laundering cocaine money through the ever more lucrative real estate market; one fellow's sales technique consisted of plying out-of-town customers with dumb dust, flying in call girls to service them, and then flogging them pieces of the old ranches up on the mesas, bought for a song, subdivided, and glorified with names like Starfire Executive Retreats, Legends of the Rockies Rancherias, and Elk Pond Estates.

Among this second wave was Kyle Croesus, an affable Texas-born-and-bred bidnessman who fancied himself, like so many of his kind, a Gentleman Hunter. His second hunting season in Telluride, Croesus was driving back to town across Turkey Creek after showing an old mining claim above Ophir to a client from Phoenix.

"It's the perfect spot for your second home," Croesus had told the man. "Jest look at the amenities. You got the best views in the San Juans. You got year-round access—see, the county has to plow the road in once there's a house here, that's the law." He lowered his voice conspiratorially, as if the camp robber jays in the trees were in the employ of rival realtors. "Just between you and me, I showed Tom Cruise this place just last week. It was love at first sight. But he told me Nicole has to see it before he buys it, and she's shooting a movie over in Spain right now." He laughed, "It don't matter if you're Tom Cruise or you and me, I guess, you still got to ax the wife!"

When Croesus dropped the client off at his rental car down at the Ophir Loop, he added a little more myth to grease the wheels. "Ya know, it's breakin' my client's heart to sell. This claim's been in the family since 1889. His great-granddaddy was one of the original White Men in San Miguel County. He's a proud man, but the family's, well, they're kinda cash-poor right now," this last "fact" in that same don't-tell-a-soul lowered voice.

In reality, the client was a Denver-based corporation called Prodigian Associates that specialized in buying up old mining claims and national forest and park inholdings at tax sales, jacking up the price, and selling them off. Prodigian had paid $778.23 for this one, and Croesus was instructed not to let it go for less than $1.2 million.

Not only that, the place was inaccessible seven months out of the year; the county would plow the trail up Ajax Peak before they ploughed this particular piece of back road. And the property lay smack in the runoff zone of one of the biggest avalanche chutes in Swamp Canyon. Plus, if the EPA ever got around to analyzing the torrent of goo that poured out of the old mine tunnel, the place would be a prime candidate for a Superfund site. If the EPA inspectors didn't keel over from the radon fumes rising from the mine tailings first.

And, of course, the closest Croesus had ever been to Tom Cruise was when he and his wife, Charolais, rented *Mission Impossible.*

Real estate, as Croesus liked to say, wasn't all about location, location, location, it was fabrication, fabrication, fabrication.

And it worked. The man from Phoenix was his, hook, line, and sinker. He could feel it.

Now, as Croesus drove south across Turkey Creek in the fine afternoon light, he spied something in the pastures off to the left, something that made him jam on his brakes. He pulled off the highway, turned off the ignition, and got his .30–06 from the back seat. He always carried the .30–06, loaded and ready to fire. You never knew when you were going to run into something worth shooting: a red-tailed hawk on a fence post; a couple of young bobcats playing in the sun; a coyote, hunting for food for her pups.

Well, this was better than that: the biggest bull elk he had ever seen, with antlers the size of a chandelier, just standing there in the field like he owned it.

What a great day, Croesus told himself.

He crept along the fence line, with its No Hunting and Private Property—No Trespassing signs, till he was less than two hundred feet from the big bull. Who just kept standing there, re-joicing silently in the afternoon.

You dumb bastard, Croesus thought. You're gonna look just right on my rec room wall.

Croesus raised the rifle to his shoulder, aimed, and fired.

An hour later, he pulled up in front of the liquor store on Main Street in Telluride, the huge, bloody elk's head tied to his front bumper so everyone could see. He went into the store, got a bottle of the Famous Grouse off the shelf, and paid for it with his Visa Gold. When he came back out, three local kids, ten, eleven years old, were standing there, staring at the trophy head.

"Really sumpin', huh?" he grinned expansively. "One shot. One shot, and—Bye-bye!"

The kids looked at him, their eyes tight, bright, their faces bloodless.

Then one of them, a girl with close-cropped, streaked blond hair in a THS sweatshirt and red, yellow, and green Rasta beads, spoke up.

"You killed our elk, you fat motherfucker," she said.

"Your elk? Hey, listen—"

But they didn't listen. The three of them turned and walked away. When they were fifty feet away or so, they turned, and all three gave him the finger, before continuing on their way.

A couple of autumns ago, a black bear sow and her twin cubs were raiding the dumpsters and garbage cans on the north side of town, below Tomboy Road. That part of Telluride is known as Sunnyside, due to its south-facing, sloping terrain. Because it catches measurably more hours of sunlight per day than the rest of town, and because of the large number of grand, Victorian-era homes there, it has become a neighborhood for the wealthy, most of them newcomers who can pay 2.2 million cash without blinking for a house they are going to inhabit only a few months out of the year at most. Many of them feel that their wealth gives them the right to remake "their" mountains to fit their paltry fantasies and petty desires.

The three bears didn't fit into the vision of certain of these nimrods. Instead of locking up their garbage and bear-proofing their decks and porches, they demanded that Something Be Done. So Something Was. The authorities tranquilized the mother bear and dumped her, sans cubs, a couple of hundred miles away on the Uncompahgre Plateau. And when she returned a few days later, frantic to find her cubs, they shot and killed her under Colorado's barbaric "Two strikes and you're out" bear policy.

One of the cubs vanished. The other, too young to forage and den for the winter on her own, wandered defenseless through town. The town marshals pursued her with drawn guns and speeding cop cars. The town's myriad roving dogs joined in the hunt. Finally, in broad daylight, the terrified little cub climbed a power pole, touched a hot wire, and was electrocuted.

I called Town Hall the next day, to find out where the body was. I had the crazy idea that others in Telluride were as appalled as I was, that perhaps we could organize a procession with the bear's body and an appropriate burial in Town Park. Perhaps in death the bear could help teach the human beings here that living in the mountains is not a free ride, and that our sloppy, care-less lives have tragic consequences for this place we so loudly profess to cherish.

But no one knew what had happened to the corpse. "Maybe they hauled it to the dump," the official phone voice said in a tone that suggested infinite uninterest. No one wrote a letter to the newspaper or dropped by "KOTO News" to do a guest com-mentary on a Mountain Town that cut its own heart out so casu-ally and threw it away.

Ghost Stories

No wonder there are so many ghosts here in the San Juan country, where so much has been lost or destroyed. Anyone who's spent much time out here has his or her share of strange tales: ghosts, afreets, djinns, haints, things going bump in the night, weird ectoplasmic happenings.

In Telluride itself, it's a well-known fact that both the Sheridan Opera House and the old Pick & Gad building have their resident haunts. Lone Tree Graveyard, aka the Marble Orchard, is a veritable gated community of spooks. Some spots in the San Juans are haunted in a sinister, seemingly malign, way. I wouldn't spend a night alone in that old miners' boarding house up in La Junta Basin if you paid me. There's just something about the place, an echo of long-dead insane laughter that hangs around in the air there, as if it's waiting.

Fool's Gold

Deserts seem to be naturally linked with death and the Dead.
Back in 1274, Marco Polo described how travelers crossing the
Gobi were led astray by spirits. If one were separated from the
caravan at night, Polo wrote, "when he tries to gain his company
again he will hear spirits talking, and will suppose them to be his
comrades. Sometimes the spirits call him by name; and thus shall
a traveler oft times be led astray so that he never finds his party.
And in this way many have perished. Even in the day-time one
hears those spirits talking."

"Do you ever feel, when you're looking at one of those pic-
tographs or petroglyphs, in some lonesome canyon, that a big
hand's gonna come out of the rock, grab you, and pull you in?" an
Anasazi rock art expert once asked me rhetorically, in a cafe in
Bluff, Utah. "Into Rock Land, or Anasazi Time, or whatever
there is down under there? A place where those big blank-faced
gods rule, along with the spirits of animals, and man is not the
master anymore?"
    "I thought you were supposed to be a scientist," I kidded her.
    "That doesn't mean I'm a fool," she laughed. She took a hit of
coffee. "Just look at something like the Green Mask, or the Procession Panel. I approach them like an electrician working
around a 100,000-volt socket. Very carefully."
    There's always been a ghosty feel to those canyons where the
Anasazi, ancestors of today's Pueblo Indians, lived. To those
abandoned cliff dwellings, and the enigmatic figures of men,
gods, beasts, and monsters painted on the rocks or incised into

the sandstone. You walk softly down there, if you are wise, and watch your step.

Recent archaeological revelations, that some Anasazi groups practiced mass cannibalism and literally cooked and devoured their "enemies" (outsiders, strangers) only add to the sense that one is in constant peril down in those rock mazes: that the Deads are watching you, waiting for their chance.

I recall a trip down Big Gulch years ago with my pal Trumbull. This was back in the old, empty days, before the gulch had that many visitors. It was autumn, and the cottonwoods were yellow; you could feel winter on the air, a foreboding chill.

The third day out, we came upon a spooky little side canyon guarded by a huge boulder with an eerie petroglyph scratched in its varnished side: the figure of some kind of horned werebeast, standing triumphantly atop a human being.

I decided to explore up the side canyon while Trumbull hiked on down the main gorge.

You lose track of time in the desert. I don't know how long I scrambled up the slick rock ledges, through pools of dry sand, climbing the sinuous sandstone corridor, but before I knew it, the day was waning, the shadows lengthening, deepening. I didn't want to get caught up there in the dark. It was time to head back, pronto.

That's when it happened. I distinctly heard Trumbull, somewhere farther up the side canyon, calling me. Weird, since I couldn't figure out how he could have gotten from the main canyon to the upper part of the side canyon without me seeing him. Still, I called back: "Yeah, hey, Trumbull. That you?"

No response, except for that voice, insistently calling my name—Rob, Rob. A voice out of nowhere.

I very nearly decided to follow the voice, but something didn't make sense to me. I paused. Yeah, how the hell *did* Trumbull get up there, and why didn't he respond when I called back? It not only didn't make sense, but I didn't like *how* it didn't make sense. I started back down, away from the mysterious voice, away from whatever it was that lurked up in those farther shadows.

When I arrived at the mouth of the side canyon and scrambled past the sinister glyph-marked boulder down to the main canyon floor, I ran right into Trumbull. Before I could say a word, he beat me to it. "Hey, where were you?" he asked.

"What do you mean?"

"Was that you, down in the main canyon?" He indicated the direction from where he had come.

I felt the creepy-crawlies at the back of my neck. "Not me."

"Well, I heard you. I didn't see you, but I heard you. You kept calling my name. But every time I looked for you, it was like you were just ahead of me, one more turn down the canyon."

"Ah. That's not so good."

"It wasn't you? Joking around or something?"

"It wasn't me. I heard you, up where I was. You were yelling to me."

We looked at each other.

Trumbull finally spoke. "Let's get back to camp."

It was the kind of night when you sleep with your back to the rock, one hand on your headlamp and the other on your Russian surplus bayonet.

Another time, I ran into a group of archaeologists down in the canyons. All women, from some place like Northern Arizona University, they were excavating an Anasazi trash midden filled with burial sites along Spider Creek. I ate dinner with them one night, at their base camp, and one of them told me the following story:

"I got back to base camp from the dig around dusk, when I realized I'd left my watch back down at the midden. I decided to go back and get it. It took me about twenty minutes to get back down there, hurrying. I was down in the pit, putting on my watch, when I heard someone coming. They were singing softly, in some language I didn't know.

"I don't know why, but I felt terrified. I crouched down there in the hole as the singer approached. I made myself look up. There was the silhouette of a woman, against the dark cliff, and she was singing to me. I felt like I'd swallowed a block of ice.

"After a few minutes the ghostly figure retreated, and there was silence in the canyon. I jumped out of the dig and ran all the way back to camp. I think I made it in about seven minutes flat!

"The thing was, the grave I was digging, where I left my watch, there was a woman buried there. I think it was her, that came and sang to me. I'd disturbed her rest, and she was warning me, telling me to leave her alone. The next morning I got up early, went back down to the dig, and covered up her bones, reburied her. It seemed the right thing to do—and the wise thing, too.

"I think maybe I'll give up archaeology. Digging up other people's dead, it can't be good. Who knows what the Old Ones left behind down there? Whatever it is, it's none of our business."

And then there was the time, down in one of the left-hand side canyons of Slickhorn. Also autumn, also empty. Four of us hike a day down into the gorge. The place is eerily dry, after a summer of even less rain than usual. We plod through the fine sand left by pools, clamber down dry waterfalls and pour-offs. At last, where the canyon bottoms out and meets a smaller tributary ravine, we find a pool of antique water with a thin skin of cottonwood leaves on top. Dirty water, old water, stale water: it doesn't matter out here, where Water equals Life.

We set up camp on a sandy ledge system above the pool, beneath a gigantic totemic cottonwood, and start exploring our neighborhood. A few minutes later Tad, our resident climber, yells triumphantly that he's found something, something Big. We drop whatever we're doing and hurry down canyon to meet him.

There he is, perched atop a top-heavy twenty-foot boulder. The way up there isn't that easy, but with some coaching from above we manage, through a series of artless and brute-force acrobatics, to join him.

The top of the boulder is a sloping ramp about fifteen feet square. And its desert-varnished surface is covered, like a rough-hewn blackboard, with a tableau of petroglyphs: vague humanoids, demi-whatsises, signs and symbols, crazy stars, and zoomy flying objects.

I'm sure no one had seen this panel of sacred art since it was scratched in the varnished sandstone over a thousand years ago. These potent images were not created for human eyes: they are aimed at the sky, like those far larger magical forms scratched out of the surface of the Atacama Desert in Peru. And it's pure chance we found them. This canyon is chock-full of boulders like this; Tad chose to climb this particular dolmen by pure chance . . . I guess. Who really knows?

The sun goes down soon after we climb down off the rock. It's a bright blazing night, lit by a full moon. The air is warm and still.

Sometime around midnight I awake. To a sound—a very, very strange sound. Something between the bleating of a sheep and the cry of a bird. And it's coming from just outside our tent.

I crawl out of my sleeping bag and look around. There are the embers of our campfire; there's the other tent, fifty feet away on a slightly higher ledge. The bare cottonwood looms over us, brilliant silver. But nothing else. And the sound keeps coming.

First it's over here, then it's over there. I pursue it, thinking—what? A lost lamb? A wounded hawk? I have no idea that makes sense. And though I look and look . . . nada, nothing.

"What are you doing out there?" Nancy calls from our tent.

"Don't you hear that?"

"Of course I hear it. What is it?" Being awakened in mid-sleep ranks low on her list of favorite things.

"I don't know. The damn thing is invisible."

A rude chuckle from Nancy.

My daughter calls from the higher tent. "What's that noise?"

"I don't know," the Intrepid Investigator replies. "That's what I'm trying to find out!"

Finally, I give up, only to be awakened, again and again, by the phantom call. Again and again I go out into the night. I look everywhere.

It's not the echo of a frog. I've heard that before. And it's not frog season, dammit! It's a ventriloquizing sheep . . . a Royal Nonesuch . . . a Desert Yeti with a sense of humor.

No, it's a Ghost. Roused when we climbed onto that forbidden, hidden rock and gazed upon those ancient messages not meant for us.

San Juan Miracles

Hiking up Bear Creek, solo, summer. In the Upper Wasatch Basin, tundra valley studded with Andy Goldsworthy–like boulders. No one on the trail today. The ground littered with bits of stone coated with thousands of the tiniest quartz crystals. I pick up one especially fine piece and then, on an impulse, leave a dollar in a cup-shaped depression atop one of the boulders. A trade, with the Big Gods who watch from inside the mountains.

On the way back down, late that afternoon, on impulse I stop and shinny up the boulder where I left the dollar.

The money's gone; in its place is a big cobble of the crystal-coated rock, the best I've ever seen, twinkling like diamonds.

* * *

Spring, Lizard Head Pass. A full-moon night, warm, chinook weather. I'm cross-country skiing up there with a friend, Samantha Adams. The snow burns like white-hot coals. It hisses beneath our skis. Sheep Mountain glows against the stars. We stop, and sit down under a tree, on a bed of pine needles and duff.

"I wonder where the coyotes are," Samantha says.

That very instant, a coyote howls from the woods behind us. Another joins it, and then another. Answered a moment later by a whole pack of them, over toward Trout Lake. And then more coyotes join in from across the road, up toward Lizard Head Rock. There must be two dozen of them at least, and they don't stop singing. They're still at it when we ski back down an hour later and start driving back to town.

Summer. Dawn. J. Michael Brown is walking his dog out by the beaver pond when he hears a strange sound in the sky, a mighty susurration of feathers, sinews, whispers. Without warning, a flock of white pelicans drops down and lands on the water. He's lived here as long as I have, and he's never seen anything like it. He watches the birds for a while, and then walks back into town.

He's going down Main Street as the first rays of the sun shine from over the peaks at the head of the valley. A few other people are walking around, getting coffee, loading lumber in trucks, opening up offices and shops. Suddenly, someone yells and points. Everyone looks up, as the pelicans, in perfect formation, fly down Main Street a hundred feet up, heading west. When they reach the edge of town, they rise into the sky and slowly vanish, never to be seen again.

San Juan Miracles

* * *

Winter. A big storm just broke, dumping a foot or two, and now it's cold and clear. My friend Trumbull and I close down the Senate Bar and decide to take our skis up Bear Creek Road. We meet at three A.M., and head on up, illuminated by a million stars.

Powder avalanches are spin drifting down off the crags on both sides as we break trail up to the base of the Wasatch Trail. Then we decide to keep going: it's just too beautiful to stop.

We galumph up the Wasatch, climbing clumsily in our old wooden x-c skis, up into Wasatch Basin. It looks a little too avalanchey to continue from there; plus, our feet are getting cold. We head down, thrashing through snow-covered thickets, grabbing onto trees to make emergency stops, a truly ugly exhibition of back country timber bashing.

We've stopped to catch our breath on the bottom stretch of the Wasatch, gazing silently at the micaceous powdered sugar and silver world around us. I'm looking at the big cliff face opposite us, to the southeast. Tiny snowslides are sifting down everywhere. And then I realize that a light is blinking at me, from up there in those near-vertical rocks. It's like someone signaling, in some code I cannot read. Then another light is blinking, somewhere else on those frozen cliffs. When it stops, another starts in. And so on. A myriad of mysterious lights, shining down, spelling out . . . something.

I must be imagining things. Then I look over at Trumbull.

"You see those—?" he says.

"Lights. Yeah."

"I thought I was imagining things."

"Me too."

The lights keep on shining, shifting, trying to tell us something.

I have been reading about owls all this last year. Ever since I disturbed an ancient owl's nest in a sacred Indian cave above the Salton Sea in the Sonoran Desert of California. When I drove back to Telluride last winter in a blizzard at two A.M., a Great Horned Owl was sitting on the highway sign at the crest of Keystone Hill. Waiting for me. As I drove past, he suddenly took wing, grazed the snow-covered hood of my car with one great pinion, leaving a slash of a signature across the white, and vanished into the storm.

Now, on a freeze-out January day, I'm hiking in Grand Gulch. It's sub-sub-zero, the midday sky cruelly clear, the air stabbing like tiny shiatsu needles in my nostrils.

"I wish I would see an owl," I say under my breath, and at that instant something enormous explodes from a cleft in the canyon wall and flies over me, actually touching me. It happens so quickly, with such surprise, that I can't really see what it is. But a feather drifts down in its wake and lands in the icy trail two steps in front of me: the unmistakable barred feather, moonlight and shadow, from an owl's wing.

The mountains are not dead things, they are very much alive. We try and kill them, with mines, roads, ski trails, lifts; and they keep trying to talk to us, before it's too late.

There are many, many more miracles; but this is enough, I think.

Summertime

A h, the everyday ecstasies of the mountains!

The ski area is too big. The bighorns are gone, chased into extinction by deerhounds let loose by some of my fellow émigrés. There are still mountain lions around, up on the Highline Trail and Wilson Mesa, but none on the ski mountain—too many people there now.

But still . . .

Saturday morning, 6:45. I peer out the window: the skies are gray and muddled. Leftover rain from last night is plinking and dribbling off the eaves. Down valley, shreds of cloud hang over the cliffs and the valley walls, a landscape out of a Chinese Sung Dynasty scroll.

It smells like rain, feels like rain, tastes like rain: more like the Sierra Madre Occidental, Thailand, or Oregon than the typical crispy-fried air and King Tut skies of a southwestern Colorado summer. This summer it's been pouring for weeks. Unusual, but then unusual is usual here in the San Juans. If it snows on the Fourth of July and Christmas dawns to a dust-laden simoom, hey, it's all part of the package. If you want predictability, move to (shudder) L.A., or the Biodome.

By nine-thirty it's time to hit the high country. If anything, the skies are darker, more menacing, the clouds denser. But if we don't go now, we're not going at all. Driving south across Turkey Creek Mesa we get a fine view of impending storm. The Wilsons have wrapped themselves in a dark gray blanket of Garbo-like disdain. Shrouds of evanescent mist, what the Navajos call Female Rain, hang in the skies off toward Utah. More gloomious masses of black wrath jostle for position off toward the east and southeast, grumbling and muttering.

And it's beautiful. The forests have never looked so green, the meadows so dense, the wildflowers so brilliant with waterlogged colors. It's a darkness that shines, for those of us crazy enough to be out in it. We happy few, we may get struck by lightning, or catch pneumonia, but it's worth it.

We settle for a ramble up above Ophir, up Waterfall Canyon. We park the car by Paul Machado's house and clamber down the slope to the stream. Cross over on a slippery log and start up the narrow track through the steep forest. The woods are going crazy this year with mushrooms, lichens, cloud ears and mosses, threads and bulbs, chessmen, miniature terrestrial coral gardens, lewd tuberosities that look like items from a Pleasure Chest catalog, scalloped whoziwhatsises like the clouds in a Tibetan thangka, as the great silvery Internet of mycelium that underlays the forest floor fires off everything in its arsenal.

We pick about a pound and a half of boletes on our way up, to accompany a couple of steaks we have stashed away at home. This summer we've been eating wild mushrooms breakfast, lunch, and dinner, mostly chanterelles but sometimes boletes.

Whoah! There, growing out of a midden of gray gravel, is a big old *Amanita muscaria,* like an upside-down, red, 100-watt light-bulb freckled with white, perfect for that pagan Christmas tree. Eat it and you'll have visions, and maybe die in agony in the process. Better find yourself some sheep droppings or cowpies with Rocky Mountain varieties of *Psilocybe cubensis* sprouting from their tops. One of the local witch doctors filled her hat with them over by Norwood last week and handed them out in the saloons.

The forest smells a hundred thousand years old, timeless. Ah, the treasures of the Ice Age Aftermath we were lucky enough to be born into! Not to mention our luck at living in such a rare mountain niche, a cleft of snowmelt and beaver-created oasis in these desert ranges.

A whizzbang of lightning up toward Lizard Head, a sharp crack of thunder . . . paradise, indeed. Stiff Patterson has red columbines growing out of his front walk right in downtown Telluride, through the cracks in the concrete! Up Eider Creek, you can smell the licorice, pine-tar funk of elk where their migration routes cross the trail.

Last week we just managed to reach the summit of Ajax Peak and start down before a lightning storm bombarded the high screefields. Today we're down low enough to avoid lightning, but the weather still nails us. First the forest begins to roar all around us. Then the rain hits, in a solid mass. We're wearing "waterproof" clothing, Gore-Tex in Nancy's case, some oilskin-nylon blend in mine, but we may as well be buck naked. Within five minutes we're soaked. And cold: each drop of this mountain rain contains a grain of ice, a diamond. Put it under the microscope, and it's easy to imagine you'd see one of those wintry scenes in a plastic ball: tiny people, dancing in a forest white with hoar.

By the time we make it back down to the car, our skin is gray with mild hypothermia. The clouds have devoured the mountainsides overlooking Ophir; the roof of the sky has fallen in. As we drive home, rocks are plummeting down onto the highway, loosened by the deluge.

Just before it sets the sun emerges. It keeps raining, raining fire, and a rainbow appears over the Telluride Valley. Another rainbow appears inside it. Then another. Then a fourth. People come out into Main Street from the bars, shops, and offices, whooping and hollering. The mountains appear through the clouds, shimmering with fresh snow on their tops. They are lit with an ethereal red glow.

Then it all goes dark. It keeps raining all night long.

This is why we live here. The golden steam rising from mushrooms in the pan, the cold rain shattering on the roof, a soft roar like the sea.

Forecast for Monday: Hail, thunderstorms, sunny, partly cloudy, mostly cloudy, highs in the 90s, lows between 10 and 20, winter storm warning, flash flood watch, high winds, no winds.

Hiked up to Hope Lake the other day, and it did everything but rain toads and generate sand dunes. First it was hot and sunny, then it rained, hot and sunny again, then cold rain and wind, then (yep) sunny, then a deluge of hail mixed with grapnel hurled on a maelstrom, accompanied by a thunder-and-lightning show disturbingly reminiscent of a mortar barrage I experienced on a ridgeline in Kunar, Afghanistan, a few years back. And then, whilst we skidded and slewed our way back down the mudded-up trail, the sun again, the air languid, humid, and thick down in the jungly forest.

We looked around at the bright, tranquil mountains, and they all had innocent smiles on their faces, as if to say, "Who, us??"

And it all happened in three hours and change.

The San Juans are infamous for their quirky, quakey, tricky-dicky weather, but this summer has been exceptional. First we had a huge onslaught of late, wet snow. Then we got rain, oceans of it. Then a mini-drought, with the usual Forest Fire Danger alerts. I had to water the rocky hillside we call our garden every day.

And now, we've got the Second Coming of the Great Flood. It rains and rains, and then it rains some more.

After the amphibious assault on Hope Lake, we decided to go down valley to a party at the Buddhist's house in Placerville. The Buddhist is a small, ferocious Nissei who works as a carpenter summers and does avalanche control work in winter. That turned into a meteorological epic, too. Reports came in on the radio: Keystone Hill closed by mudslide. Dallas Divide closed by Leopard Creek overflow. Norwood Hill closed. More mud-and-debris slides hitting Sawpit and Fall Creek.

We set out in the old four-wheel-drive Ford anyhow and made it to Placerville via a dogleg down the Ames-Ilium Road. Sawpit looked like a mud-bomb had hit it as we drove through at dusk: a mud-bomb studded with king-sized boulders. Fall Creek was a beachhead. Holy mountain mackerel. Every second you half expected Thor or Ullr or Coyote or whoever truly rules these ranges to hurl down another big old rock and, blotto!

When we drove home, the main highway was open again, but barely. We crept between boulders and mounds of debris, illuminated by cops' flashlights and strobing emergency red-&-blues.

The next morning was mostly sunny. By afternoon it was raining again. The National Weather had another Flash Flood Alert out for the whole Four Corners area.

The stories coming in from down valley about the previous night's tsunami were awesome. One friend of ours was trying to reinforce her fence when she saw her next-door neighbor's car floating toward her property line. Several houses were saved at the last second when Sheriff Bill Masters brought out inmate volunteers from the county jail down in Ilium and led them in a shovel brigade.

Well, what else is new? In the past, spring runoff and microburst thunderstorms created two gigantic deluges. In 1909 the dam containing Trout Lake, south of town and a valley over, gave way under a big snowmelt and the whole crashed down Ilium Valley, devouring all in its path. The famous Ames Power Plant, where the genius young engineers from Cornell known as the Pinheads had introduced alternating current to the world in the 1890s, was annihilated. According to the legend, the Pinheads saved themselves by calculating exactly how much water was descending toward them, how fast and deep. Then they climbed power poles just high enough to stay out of the flood waters: no use in wasting energy, after all. Their calculations were so exact that the water just grazed the soles of their shoes.

In 1914, after a freak thunderstorm south of Telluride, a monster flood of water, mud, rocks, and uprooted trees came roaring down Coronet Creek, inundating much of the town in chest-deep alluvium and killing one local woman. As Senior Mahoney, crusty ex-miner and amateur meteorologist, says, "If you don't like the weather in the San Juans, just wait five minutes and it'll change."

There's a reason 99.99999 percent of the human race doesn't live up this high. By "this high," I mean the altitude zone encompassed by Telluride, Ophir, Leadville, and a couple of other Colorado Rocky Mountain burgs: circa 9,000 feet above sea level, in the thin, cold air. And the reason is, because summers are briefer than a butterfly's dream up here. Intensely, flamingly beautiful, but short. It definitely takes getting used to, living up where summer is a footnote, autumn an afterthought, and winter rules. It takes gumption, toughness, adaptability.

Consider our cousin, the good ol' Colorado-variety black bear. In lower, mellower, warmer, and more fecund climes, black bears don't hibernate at all; they don't need to. A little higher up, where it's cooler and there's less year-round food, they snooze for maybe three, four months out of twelve. Down in Mexico, the few *osos negros* not shot out by ranchers don't hibernate at all.

Fool's Gold

But up here, our gnarly timberline/screefield/krummholz bruins spend more than half of their lives asleep, comatose. What a mad lifestyle: 6.5 months of the year, October through March, they sleep in a hole in the ground; the other 5.5 months they eat like ambulatory dumpsters, anything they can wrap their jaws around, fueling up for the next Big Sleep: bugs, carrion, grass, bark, pine cones, honey, moss.

At a recent Telluride Bluegrass Festival, a black bear tore open a metal cooler and devoured two pounds of baloney and a cheese wheel and a six-pack of Coors it found inside. Another recent summer, a local drove back from Montrose City Market with a big load of groceries and decided to leave them in his Jeep overnight and unload them in the morning. The poor fellow lived at the base of Tomboy Road, favorite bear-prowling territory. When he got up in the morning, the rear door of his Jeep had been ripped off its hinges, and the guilty bear responsible had eaten all the food.

But back to the subject at hand.

All those musty old-timers' jokes about the guy who went down to Denver on the last day of spring for the weekend and came back Sunday night to find it was the first day of fall, they've got a bitter core of true rue in the center. It actually is possible to miss summer up in the high country. Work overtime a couple or three weeks, get a camping trip rained out, a shopping expedition to Grand Junction, and before you know it the aspens are changing and you've barely done any of the summer hikes you'd planned—Lizard Head, the Highline, Silver Lake, Wilson—those classic ritual walkabouts that help hold the year together.

116

And that's truly a bummer. You need summer up here to make it through the winter, and that's no joke. Misspend summer, and you may just find yourself come February with a bad schnapps habit, poaching Prozac to try and keep from tumbling into the Pit.

These high-altitude summers are absolutely, indubitably the sweetest, the best in the world. They may be short, but they pack a thousand times more punch than the longer, easier, lazier summers you get down on the flatlands. It's almost like they shouldn't, couldn't be any longer than they are. Like a shooting star, a bolt of lightning, or ice crystals on a cabin window, their beauty is inextricably tied to their evanescence. The bicycle-bell jingling of ruby throats, the smell of rain, the sumptuous gardens of columbines with butterflies waltzing through them, the stands of aspen glowing in the dusk like green candles . . . it's all too much.

Last week I was tromping around up in one of the high basins that overhang the Telluride Valley. It was hot and sunny, the wildflowers were blazing: a Midsummer Day's Daydream come true. I waded a snowmelt torrent, and a half hour later my shoes were dry again.

An hour later, as I hiked back down the akimbo meadowlands, a posse of scowling thunderheads sauntered out from behind the Wilsons. The sky darkened, thunder rumbled; rain began to pelt down, and a cold wind came whooping out of nowhere. Yikes!

You know what it felt like: yep, fall, if not winter.

When I reached the timberline, there were patches of yellow leaves here and there among the high aspens. Summer, *pericoloso*.

Rock of Ages

Deep in the mountains is a strange marketplace,
where you can trade the hassles of everyday life
for eternal ecstasy.

—*Milarepa*

Strange things happen when you head out alone into the mountains. Strange wonderful, strange scary, strange awesome.

Why? I think it's for the same reason that shamanistic initiations and vision quests are carried out solo. Because there's a silent voice in the wilderness that we hear only when no one else is around. When you go far, far beyond, out across the netherlands of the Known, the din of human static slowly fades away, over and out.

119

One autumn morning, I decide to hike up over Rock of Ages Pass. No one else wants to go. But soon the first snows will close down those back basins and trails up around the Wilsons. Fortune favors the brave, and Time waits for no man. I've been meaning to do Rock of Ages all summer, and I don't want to spend the winter bumming because I never made it.

I pack a daypack with anorak, wool cap, gloves, water bottle, bananas, a sandwich, and Diet Cokes, and take my ski pole walking stick, the ultimate trekking tool. Gas up the Ford, and head out. Down into Ilium Valley and up the switchbacks onto Sunshine Mesa. Many of the aspens have lost their leaves, but there's still plenty of gold and saffron shimmering against the darkening skies.

I park the Ford at the end of the road and start walking. Sunshine Peak broods overhead to my left. As the trail climbs, I look down on my right into vast basins of timber and meadow. There's a tiny creek down there with more trout than water in it, where the right fly pulls in a fish a minute. I watched Jeff Price catch enough for a big family dinner there last summer.

While he fished and I loafed, the backcountry Forest Ranger Dunkelberger passed by, on his way from Woods Lake across to Sunshine. He'd just seen a bobcat up the lost draw that runs up into the forested base of Wilson Peak from there.

Then he was gone, on his way. Jeff and I stayed until the sun sank.

Every trail here leads back into memories. Twenty-plus years ago Renn and I came this way, over from Lizard Head Pass. We were supposed to meet George G., who was fishing up there and was going to give us a ride back to town, but George never turned up. We crisscrossed the mesa looking for him in vain, while chorales of coyotes howled at us from all sides, and ended up long after dark stumbling down the obscure road off the prow of the mesa to the San Miguel River and the main highway. It was a brilliant, starry night, this same time of year, and cold. We were standing by the road, shivering and freezing, when the Roadhawg came speeding up from his ranch in Norwood in his pickup, late for his KOTO country-and-western deejay gig, and gave us a ride to town.

A mixed-up, screwed-up day, and one of the best I've lived in my entire life. Why is it we remember, and treasure, the ordeals and quickly forget the times when all goes according to plan, on time? Does some part of us, Neolithic, hunter-gatherer, nomad, long for a long ago time when we lived our whole lives like that, wind in the face, intense, sniffing out the trail and spying out the lay of the land? Remember, we lived tens of millions of years that way, whereas our life as a farmer began less than ten thousand years ago, as Industrial Age, mechanical man less than two centuries ago, and, as for Man.com, he's been around only half a decade.

Which means . . . what? Well, I wouldn't take that computer screen you're locked into too seriously, if I were you. We're all still stone hunters, at heart. Maybe that's why we're so damned unhappy, squashed into our corporate cubicles and straitjacket jobs, squeezed into cages that, no matter how luxurious they may seem, are cages nonetheless.

"A box to put the biped in," as Gary Snyder says.

Imagine staying at the Essex House, in a penthouse suite, for free. Now imagine staying there for free, and not being allowed to leave for the rest of your life: No Exit.

That's the twenty-first century: enjoy.

Onward, toward Rock of Ages.

At the old avalanche- and storm-wrecked mine, I turn left, south, up Bilk Creek. The mountains crowd in on both sides. The trail burrows through big dank timber, across windrows of fallen logs, following the stream up. Waterfalls and rapids plummet and boom. I'm feeling empty, hollow. I stop, eat a banana, feel the jolt of sugar and sodium, and go on.

Soon the trail climbs out of the forests into the tundra. Scree slopes rise steeply on either side. Starting to get somewhere now—a good thing, too, as clouds are rolling down the mountainsides toward me. This is going to be a storm, a real one, no doubt about it. But there's no way I'm going to turn around, not today. I don't know exactly where I'm going, but wherever it is, I'm getting there.

Some days you just have that attitude that nothing's going to stop you, you can walk through weapons-grade steel and scale a hundred heartbreaking false summits; other days you just don't have it, your will power is thin soup, your very nerves and muscles lack all conviction and when your shoe comes untied the third time, you turn around and go home. Fools who have never been there themselves mistake these states for heroism and cowardice, but what they are is You, by sheer happenstance. Sometimes you eat the bear, and sometimes the bear eats you.

Rock of Ages

Sometimes you're the windshield, sometimes you're the bug. You never know.

The ski pole helps. My right knee is acting up again, and the old fractured lumbar vertebra is seizing up, knotting up my lower back and making me waddle like a duck. I dig the pole in every step or two and vault off of it, taking the strain off of my lower body. Ski-pole vaulting toward Rock of Ages, up the valley.

In the next basin, the sidetrack to the pass cuts off the main trail to Lizard Head Pass, switchbacking up through steep tundra and sloping, water-polished ledges. By the time I top out on the next level, the storm is here full force. The wind shrieks and keens, whipsawing back and forth across the fields of stone, the Gothic crags. It starts to rain.

The scene before me is uncompromisingly bleak. Below me, cupped in the depths of the cirque I have just reached, a nameless tarn, like a sheet of smoked glass, laps against banks of rubble, gravel, shattered stone. To the right, Wilson Peak gives me its cold shoulder. To the left, rotten ridgelines with no kind intentions yaw off toward Gladstone and Mount Wilson, and more morose afreets of cloud and shroud. Directly before me, beyond the gloomy pond, rises another rampart of scree and debris. Somewhere up there is Rock of Ages Pass.

Bleak, yes, but strangely it fills me with a transcendent ecstasy. This desolation is the haunt of angels and gods, prophets and saints.

I work my way around the tarn to the right, across wet, clattering, stone shingles that threaten to turn my ankle with every step. The rain comes in again, in a maelstrom so powerful that I have to stop and stand there, hunched over, and wait till it ebbs. It's hard to see, with the rain slamming down so hard, and the wind. The rain is no more than a degree or two from becoming snow.

Maybe this is it, I tell myself. The first blizzard of the year. In which case I may have to bail, after all, a discouraging thought. Which I thrust away, and start trudging upward again. No way I'm turning back now, absolutely not. I struggle, sliding, moshing and stumbling, up the steep wall of ground-up mountain to the next level, a small shelf just below the final saddle.

I take shelter in the abandoned miners' shack next to the trail and take a few minutes to dry off, warm up. The rain has slowed to a drizzle, but it's still dark, gusty. I eat the second banana, and head up the last patch.

It isn't clear exactly where the pass is: somewhere up above, in the jumble of towers, snags, and notches along the skyline. I climb up between huge teetering boulders, hand over hand. I get to the top, clinging to the slippery junk granite and peer down the other side. I'm definitely off the trail: there's no way down here, just a sheer precipice bottoming out in a break-neck boulder field below. I am lost.

More clouds are sailing in. I don't want to linger here; this is not a comfortable place.

I am working my way along the ridge, back toward Wilson Peak, when suddenly I come upon something, something strange and very disturbing. It's someone's brand-new red nylon day-pack, laid out carefully on top of a flat rock, and next to it one of those rubber-tipped aluminum hiking staffs, the high-tech equivalent of my old ski pole. Lying there, as if someone just put it there a moment ago.

I look around, expecting to see the owner sheltering in the lee of a boulder or resting. There's no one. Maybe they fell, I tell myself. I climb back up to the top of the ridge and look around. No sign of anyone. I try yelling: "Hey! HEY!" No answer. I wish I'd packed my med kit, bandages, tape, Betadine, EMT shears. I think of looking in the pack, but then I tell myself the guy's probably a hundred feet away. Searching for the trail, like me. Maybe.

I try shouting again. My voice fades away in the onrushing clouds, drowned by the wind.

Or he's up climbing Gladstone, or Mount Wilson. Bad day for it, but still. . . . I study the ridgeline that way, looking for a spot of artificial color, of Gore-Tex, Supplex, polypro. Nothing but the monotones of the rock, shattered spine of a slain dragon, and the grim peaks.

A noise: I turn and look. Something is moving. A big stone, tumbling down the slopes of Wilson Peak, smacking up rock, dust, and dirty snow—Bonk, Krump, Blomg. It descends into the void, and I feel for a dizzy instant that I am going with it.

Lightning forks in the murk down toward Navajo Lake. I inhale the hot-wire smell of electricity. Time to move.

I leave the pack and the staff where I found them. If the owner is still up here, and alive, he's going to need them.

I half climb, half fall down to where I now think the pass must be, up under Wilson Peak; and there it is.

I have three choices: Hike back the way I came, back to the car. Do the long traverse down to Navajo Lake, and up over to Woods Lake. Or take the trail that forks out over the notch between Wilson Peak and El Diente, down into Silver Pick Basin.

I decide on the last option. I recall that there are a couple of cabins there, high up, that are sometimes inhabited, and many of the folks who live that far out have cell phones or radios. I want to call in to the sheriff's office and see if anyone has been reported missing up in the Wilsons. People die up there every year, in falls, rockslides, storms.

Moving fast, I descend the rotten trail off Rock of Ages, taking two or three good falls and putting some sizable holes in my shins. Then up and over between the Scylla and Charybdis of Wilson aka Shandoka, and El Diente, the Stormmaker, and the Fang. Which are flinging rocks down right and left, a regular cannonade, and hurling lightning bolts that ignite the black hearts of the clouds. Not to mention the rain, which is coming down in near solid sheets, turning the trail to an ankle-deep trough of ice water.

I run, fall, get up, run some more. I'm out of breath, but adrenaline more than makes up for it. Down into Silver Pick, to the Jeep road and the first high homestead. Nobody home. So I keep running. Down the muddy road, in the persistent rain, punctuating my progress with more pratfalls and splats.

I keep thinking of the owner of the pack, imagining him (or her) somewhere back up in those clouds, with a broken leg, a concussion, in shock from a lightning bolt or hypothermia. That keeps me going. Once I found the pack, it was my responsibility, the weight on my shoulders. That's the way it is, up here.

I don't run into anyone till I'm way down by Many Ponies Ranch: a guy and his son, in a Jeep, on their way up to their house on the mesa. They have a cell phone and let me use it. I dial 911 and get patched through to the sheriff. They take my report and check. Nope, nobody's been reported missing up there. They get my home number and tell me they'll call if they hear anything.

The next morning, I hitch a ride back up to Sunshine and retrieve my car.

That afternoon, hearing nothing from the sheriff, I call around. Nobody at the Telluride Mountaineer knows about any local climbers up on the Wilsons: "They'd have to be crazy, in this effing weather." Search & Rescue hasn't heard anything. Charlie Fowler over in Norwood, who's brought more than one corpse down off Gladstone and Mount Wilson, ditto.

I keep asking; I even put cards up on the bulletin boards in town: "DID YOU LEAVE A RED DAYPACK UP AT THE BASE OF WILSON PEAK? IF SO, PLS. CALL—"

Nothing.

Two weeks later the first big snowstorm of the winter hits, closing down Rock of Ages, cutting it off from the rest of the world till spring.

The Great American
Underground

B eauty and mystery swing and shift all around us, in forms
ever more strange and unbelievable.

Travel southwest from Telluride and keep your eyes
peeled. In time, you'll begin to see signs pointing toward the Underground: a Paul Klee trapdoor, a shadow on a cliff that turns
into a hole, a tunnel leading down, down, DOWN . . . different
entrances to the last world before this one, beneath the oil slick
rainbows and accidental runestones of corrosion: ant trails, spider holes, Jungian bungholes, and rattlesnake railroads, leading
back down to that purer, wiser world.

This particular exit route begins with an insignificant-looking gully cutting into the dry cattle-trampled chaparral along the Utah-Arizona border. A plain old erosion gully with crumbling walls, nothing special. I wouldn't have given it a second look, but we are following directions given to us by a diehard desert-rat friend who knows all the secret routes out here.

The gully descends slowly but steadily: first it's six feet deep, then twelve, then twenty, thirty. The earth walls give way to sandstone; we're walking on bedrock, carpeted by alluvial pebbles and sand. Fifty feet down, eighty, a hundred; the gorge remains narrow, barely ten feet across, the sky a skinny strip of blue high above. And it just keeps going down, diving into the dark guts of the Underworld.

It's cool as a cave down here, and dark, and the air smells of stone, water, Time. The rock that surrounds us is at least 200 million years old, and the elements have scoured and scraped its surface to form the pockets of sand beneath our feet, 200-million-year-old sand. We're wading through Time, descending Time, breathing Time. The drab, sun-bleached desert surface we left behind a half hour ago already seems far, far away in another world, a separate reality.

We're in the slots, the slot canyons. Think of a canyon of surreal proportions, three or four hundred feet deep, with vertical or overhanging walls and a floor so narrow you have to go single file or even sideways to get through. Think of *Journey to the Center of the Earth*, Dante's Inferno, Coleridge's Xanadu . . . dream dreamy topography. Think of a canyon that feels like a tunnel, a cave, a sepulcher, a lost tomb. There's no real definition of a slot canyon, but you'll know one when you're in it.

The whole Colorado River Plateau, the high desert that sprawls across so much of the core of the Four Corners country, is a great Bedstone Block of mystery, with lost treasures, shrouded secrets, buried magic. Out in those intricately folded origamis of bedrock and sand there are still mesas that have never been scaled, hanging slick rock gardens no one has explored, uncharted cliff dwellings hidden away on shadowy ledges. But nowhere is the sense of the Unknown so powerful as in the slot canyons, Coyote, Spider, Buckskin, Cheesebox, Antelope, and all the rest. That's where the Heart of the Brilliant Darkness dwells . . . one of the places, anyhow. Slot canyons: play the slots, win or lose.

We're at least two hundred feet deep now, maybe more. Looking up, we see a disquieting sight: a reef of driftwood, logs the size of cannons, jammed between the rock walls fifty feet above our heads. Wouldn't want to be down here in a thunderstorm, no way. In August of 1997, eleven tourists were hiking down Antelope Canyon, outside Page, Arizona. A flash rainstorm hit, and ten minutes later a forty-foot wall of water roared down the narrow passage. Everyone drowned.

There's just no easy way out of these slots: the unrelenting walls go on for miles, smooth, without a break. And a storm doesn't even have to make a direct hit to trigger a flash flood. These canyons are surrounded by hundreds of square miles of bare rock and hard soil that gather every raindrop and funnel them all downhill. A ten-minute cloudburst ten miles away can end up as a veritable tidal wave right where you're walking. Caveat emptor.

In the late afternoon, we find a place to camp: the canyon widens into an amphitheater a hundred feet long by a hundred feet across, and there's an islet of clean white alluvial sand, maybe twenty feet above the canyon floor. Of course, if a genuine flash flood comes crashing down . . .

It's not only a nice campsite, it's the only possible campsite we've seen since we entered the canyon this morning. We pitch our tents, fire up the stove, cook up tea and Thai noodles with dried shrimp, along with pre-fab brownies. There's still a bright ribbon of sunlight along the rimrock, but down here it's a realm of deepening shadow. Muted gold, to mauve, to brooding gray. An unseen hawk cries somewhere up above, out of sight, a harsh, defiant *kraa—kraa!* For a moment the invisible bird's elongated shadow flies like a boomerang across that high stripe of sun, then vanishes as the hawk soars away.

Bats dive and dart through the dusk. A frog croaks from a secret pool somewhere down canyon. *Brackety-brack, ko-ax, ko-ax!* Our little island of headlamp-and-flashlight-light is engulfed by night. The distant ribbon of sky turns to stars as if somebody flicked a switch, but the light doesn't penetrate down here: it's up there, in the world of angels and human beings, and we troglodytes gaze on it from afar, from our Black Hole.

Is there anything better than waking up in a lost canyon? I don't think so. The surface world we left yesterday seems a million miles away now, hard to imagine. Job? Politics? Tire rotation, deadline, pants size? No way, José. Lie in the sleeping bag, half conscious, half dreaming, and listen to the silent John Cage music of the underworld. Darkness slowly, imperceptibly melds into the soft gray light of dawn. And then, somebody else is awake out there. A match struck, the whoosh of a stove flame, water burbling into a pot, and then the pungent spiky smell of unleashed coffee grounds, like a djinn unraveling from a lamp . . . it's time to rise.

By eight-thirty we're packed up and hiking again, descending farther, deeper, into ever more awesome zones. In places, the canyon is so narrow we can barely squeeze through with our packs. The cliffs rise in delicate scallops and waves, translucent as seashell at the edges. The floor of the canyon is paved with smooth pebbles and cobblestones, webbed with ripple-marked sand. I've seen the best Zen gardens in Japan and they have nothing on this place; in fact, they fall a bit short. Nature's accidents beat our arts, four out of five. Strange, but true. It's beautiful, and it's drastic.

In mid-morning we round a curve in the canyon and come upon a big pool. A really big pool. It stretches as far as we can see, two hundred feet at least, to the next turn in the canyon, and, more important, it's deep: first knee deep, then thigh deep, then waist deep. And it's cold, really cold. Painfully, teeth-clenchingly cold. I think of Joyce's description of the "scrotum-tightening snot-green sea." We forge on.

The pool goes on for the next mile. In places, it's nearly chest deep. In other places, it's clogged by tangled reefs of driftwood you have to climb under, over, through. Hard work, lugging forty-, fifty-pound packs through this amphibious realm. And we're lucky the water isn't deeper: some years, we find out later, this pool is too deep to walk through. You have to bring along an air mattress, float your pack on it, and dog paddle, pushing your gear before you like a tugboat. No joke.

But this, after all, is why we came here: because this is a place most people won't go. Space, after all, is the ultimate traveler's luxury these days. A luxury, lucky for some of us, that sweat equity buys but cash can't. We wouldn't be anyplace else on earth.

Especially when the pool finally ends, and we tromp out onto a fine little beach bathed in sunlight. We drop our packs, flop down, dig out candy bars and canteens, change to dry socks. Within half an hour the sun and the dry desert air have completely dried our clothes. We walk on into the afternoon, through warm amber light and crisp black shadows.

As dusk gathers, we come to another barrier: a bastion of huge tumbled boulders clogs the canyon floor, dropping off thirty vertical feet on the down-canyon side. At first it looks tricky, but then we find a gap between two of the boulders just big enough to squeeze through. If you scramble through the hole, you come out in another crawlspace between two rock faces. Brace yourself, feet against one side, back against the other, and shinny on down. Let go, and you drop onto the dorsal fin of another boulder, slippery, water-polished, forty-five degrees. Creep down that and you're back on the canyon floor, sandy terra firma.

At dusk, we come to the main canyon ours flows into. Neither canyon is more than ten feet wide here. The walls must be at least five hundred feet high. The mouth of the main canyon is lost in shadows; shin-deep water flows out of the darkness, on a bed of velvet mud and sand. The place feels like a Jungian subway station. I half expect an adobe A train to come rattling into view and hiss to a stop, and a Kokopelli conductor to yell, "This is the Precambrian Express, with stops in the Neolithic, Mesolithic, Paleolithic, Jurassic, and Triassic!"

A half mile down past the confluence the gorge widens, thirty, fifty, a hundred feet across. Here things are growing again: cat- and horsetails, rabbit brush, coyote willow. And, speaking of rabbits and coyotes, those familiar tracks, hunter and hunted, wend along the banks of the shallow stream.

We set up camp.

The slots are behind now. The country will slowly unfold before us from here on down. We're still a long, long way from anywhere. The nearest gas station is sixty-three miles away, to the south. The nearest bona fide town, seventy miles and change to the northeast. Three days farther down canyon there's a sleepy little ranch, and just below that the highway, back to ci-ci-civilization. We have to walk it, of course. And though I'm tired as hell already, I wouldn't (probably) have it any other way.

We're lucky to live in such big country. Link together all the journeys done and journeys planned out here: it would take forever, and I'd still be hungry for more. I'm the Man Who Broke the Bank at Monte Carlo when it comes to visions.

I Know It's Only Rock
& Roll, but Nizhoni'!

"In the Beginning was the Word," but not in the New World. On Turtle Island, it's "In the Beginning was the Song."

The Native American psalm has words, phrases, whole encyclopedias of layered meaning and miles- and aeons-thick alluvia of history, mystery, and philosophy, of course, but it is all also inextricably mingled with the sound of the prayer, divorced from any meaning. Like Sanskrit, Tibetan, Hebrew, Arabic, and Church Latin, Native American languages across their whole span, from Uto-Aztecan to Athabascan to Siouan to the most unique language family surviving among only a half dozen fever-stricken drunk wretches in a flooded forest on the Upper Ama-

137

zon in Peru (every time a language becomes extinct, and it happens a hundred times a year, imagine all of Shakespeare's plays and the entire contents of the British Museum, burning), all are liturgical. The music of the words was created by God, the gods, and reaches back up to those holy realms.

Sound itself is power. Sing something, and it is so. This is the soundtrack score for these mountains and deserts.

Here in the San Juan Mountains, we're on the northern edge of Dinetah, the Navajo homelands, and the intervening Ute reservations. There's nothing separating us from those alternate worlds except ourselves.

My old Ford has the yaws and a spavined tranny, but my friend Billy's truck is in even worse shape, blown out from too many rock-climbing expeditions to Yosemite and the West End. So we take the Ford.

I've gotten to know, over the phone, the members of Blackfire, a rock band that's sweeping the Navajo Rez and beyond. Blackfire consists of brothers Klee (vocals, lead guitar) and Clayton (drums) Benally, and sister Jeneda on bass. They have been touring as far afield as the Coasts and Europe and have been written up in the *Washington Post, Geo,* and *L'uomo Vogue.* Still, they have never left their rez roots, playing anti-gang and anti-alcohol concerts all over Navajo country, from Hummingbird and Two Grey Hills to Teec Nos Pos and Tuba City, and helping raise support for the Big Mountain Navajos displaced by yet another U.S. government land scam.

Native Americans have always been great musical syncretists and adapters. I once studied under Omer Stewart, the wild old

Jack Mormon anthropologist who became a Road Man (priest) in the peyote-eating Native American Church. Stewart described to me the fruition of two peyote songs believed to be divinely inspired by Jesus the Peyote Man.

One time, Stewart and Ute friends were on their way to a Peyote meeting in an old jalopy with a bopping, knocking carburetor. One of the Utes in the car started humming to himself, chanting along with the carburetor. That night, at the ceremony, after the eating of the dried gray-green cactus tops, the man sang the same song taught to him by the carburetor, gift from the vehicle of salvation that bore him and his friends to the sacred tepee.

Another time, Stewart attended a Peyote meeting down on the Navajo Rez, and when it came time for him to sing, found himself doing a kind of pared-down "Frère Jacques" with vaguely Uto-Aztecan–sounding lyrics. A year later, he heard a tape of a Peyote meeting far north in the Canadian Arctic, Dogribs or Caribou-Eaters, and someone was chanting his "Frère Jacques" song: it had traveled north, along with the sacramental cactus, all that way.

Laugh, but these are holy things.

With a few exceptions—Shawnee Indian Link Wray's classic rockabilly guitar hit "Rumble" a notable one—most Amerindian pop music through the fifties consisted of "forty-niner songs," basically trad chants with modern titles and themes like "Raising Old Glory on Iwo Jima," "Heartbreak Tipi," "I Don't Care If You Marry 16 Times," and "One-Eyed Ford." Down on the Papago Reservation in southern Arizona they were doing their own brand of accordion-mariachi stuff, called Chickenscratch, while the Navajos who strayed from traditional pretty much stuck to

C&W. Hip, politically aware young Native Americans might have dug Buffy Sainte-Marie, but on the big rural western rezzes she was pretty much nobody.

In the seventies, the rezzes began to rock. Key in the Southwest, where a great majority of the United States's Native American population lives, was XIT (for "Crossing of Indian Tribes"), led by Lakota singer Tom Bee. XIT, based out of Albuquerque, was truly pan-tribal: lead guitar was a young Jicarilla Apache genius named Billy Joe Banghart, while the bass player and drummer were Navajo and Pueblo guys.

XIT combined traditional music with snatches of C&W and lots o' hard rock, and lyrics about tribal politics and life. Their greatest hit, "Reservation of Education," is bueno, brilliant. With lyrics in English, Dineh'(Navajo), and Lakota, the song deals with the tragedy of forced acculturation, and then segues into a riff on racial pride and alcoholism:

> As long as they can keep us on the bottle,
> they think that they can keep us in our place.
> Look them in the face!
> Don't you take that drink—
> Don't turn out to be
> Exactly what they think—
> Don't take it, don't you take it—

I was fortunate enough to see Tom and the band do that song at a summer open-air concert at the Shiprock Rodeo Grounds ages ago, the only Anglo in a sea of whooping, shouting Navajos, and it was one of those moments of true and pure Rock & Roll

Magic, all those tough put-down high schoolers, sheepherders, Vietnam vets, singing along with Bee's fiery words, stomping their cowboy boots in solidarity (while an occasional empty beer can arced exuberantly through the night air).

"London Calling"? Try "Shiprock Calling" . . . dig it.

Today you can hear everything from Navajo rap to Navajo rock to punk, schmaltz, C&W (of course), on the rez. A few months ago I was driving from Kayenta to Teec Nos Pos, on the way home from L.A., tuned in to the hip FM station at Red Mesa High School, when BANG!, the following delightfully whack song came on, chanted—no yelled—by some group whose name I have forgotten—

ASK YOUR MOM FOR 50 CENTS
TO SEE THE FAT MAN JUMP THE FENCE—
HE JUMP SO HIGH HE TOUCH THE SKY,
DIDN'T COME DOWN TILL THE 4TH OF JULY—
HI YI YI YI, YA YA HI—

A crazy posse of Mudmen, happy Yeis from Outer Spaze . . .

So anyhow, Billy and I are off to see Blackfire. We drive south on a summer morning: over Lizard Head Pass, then following the upper reaches of the Dolores River down, and then out of the mountains. Into the tilted mesas and sandy range of the desert. Past Cortez, we are on Indian Land: first the Ute Mountain Ute Rez, and then, as we leave Colorado, over the San Juan's glistening sandbars, thickets, and roiling waters, past that Voidest of Monuments Four Corners (of what??), Dinetah, the Navajo Nation. That long hoodoo valley between Mesa Verde and Sleeping

Ute Mountain always seems to me to be the gateway between two worlds. North, the land is surveyed, spiked, and studded, nailed down with the perverse denatured signs of the White Man: "For Sale," "Vacation Homesites," "Zoned Industrial," "Private Property No Trespassing." South is Indian Country, held (at least for now) by blood, custom, clan. Turnoffs to hogans and sheep camps are marked with tires or boots on fenceposts.

Teec Nos Pos, with Rattlesnake and Biclabito to the left; we turn right, through Red Mesa, Mexican Water, Rock Point, Round Rock. The warm wind, the blowing sand, the tumbleweed (an import from Mongolia) rolling across the road, the tamarisk (another Asian immigrant) rippling along a draw, the temporary waters (from some long-gone thunderstorm miles away) slinking down stream toward Caverns. Measureless to Man, all combine to produce a sense of dreamlike surreality, like we're hardly here at all and maybe not.

Trickster Territory. Once, driving across the Chuska Mountains that rear up on our left, I picked up a Navajo hitchhiker who told me, pokerfaced, how a Yeti killed and ate his prize goat. When he saw that I actually believed him he nearly sprained his face trying not to howl with laughter, spent the rest of the ride staring out the window studiously scrutinizing the landscape, the corners of his mouth twitching despite himself. They're all wise guys down here, make no mistake about it, and Nothing is True, including these words, as they say.

Piñon bakes in the sun on the two-lane blacktop back road to Hopi. The place is jumping today: with a big rodeo and fair and a tatterdemalion flea market in addition to Blackfire. The town is filling up with trucks full of Navajos from the back country, sheep camps, and hard-scratch farms way out at the ends of nameless roads and beyond.

We pass an old, old granny in a pickup, driving about twenty miles an hour, hunched over the wheel; her bumper stickers say BAN CRIMINALS, NOT GUNS, and IF YOU LOVE SOMETHING, SET IT FREE—IF IT DOESN'T COME BACK, TRACK IT DOWN & KILL IT.

There's a .30–06 carbine with ironsights in the rack behind her head.

Blackfire isn't here yet; they're en route, from Flagstaff. This was kind of a last-minute gig for them. There was a drive-by gang shooting in Piñon last week, and the locals asked them to come, to help defuse the threatening violence. On the makeshift stage in the schoolyard Navajo Elvis is performing.

Let me try and explain Navajo Elvis. He's this weathered little guy in black who bears no resemblance at all to Original Elvis, who travels the rez performing the King's repertoire to taped backup music. He doesn't look like Elvis, and he doesn't sound much like Elvis either. Yet in some peculiar way he channels Elvis more truly than El Vez, Tortelvis, or Andy Kaufman. There's an almost total lack of irony, and yet, in true subtle equivocal Navajo style, you can't tell whether he's trying to be funny, or not, or both.

"Loving youuuu!" he sings, and drops to one knee and points out into the crowd. A row of elderly women laugh caustically. Then he tries to hop up again, but his old knees fail him: he has to grab the floor and hoist himself, clamber clumsily to his boots, fighting for balance.

But he keeps singing: song after song after song. Even after Blackfire shows up and gets ready to play, he keeps on going. And the crowd applauds while they laugh at him, laughs at him while they applaud: a kindly reaction, even among the young gang bangers with their colored bandanas and tattoos and baggy Levis, the same ones who shoot at each other and everybody else every night on the road back to Chinle.

And finally, as the parched afternoon ebbs, what we've all been waiting for.

They come out first in feathers and deer hides with their father, Jones Benally, a tiny, wrinkled man who's one of the most prominent medicine men on the Navajo Rez. They perform for about forty minutes with drums, chanting, doing the ancient swooping, shuffling dances, purifying the ground and the air.

Then they vanish from the stage.

A few minutes later the three kids, Klee, Clayton, and Jeneda, reemerge looking BAD in rock & roll black. They plug in, look at each other, and—"WOPBOPOOBOPALOPBAMBOOM!!" Radical Metal soars across the rez. Exaltation, liberation. The echoes reach all the way to the mountains to the north up the gorges, down the ridgelines, till they rattle the aspen leaves on the hillside outside my front door at home.

Sacred Waters

I am half owner of a quarter share in a raft that cost two hundred dollars twenty-two years ago. It's a twelve-foot NRS Otter that Nancy, Rita, Carol, and Connie bought third-hand. They made a crude floor for it, out of three-eighth-inch plywood, and got five cheap aluminum paddles, one for a spare. They rigged it out with cheap nylon rope and three or four battered carabiners, left over from the days when Nancy climbed.

Today, the raft consists of more patches than original rubber, but she's still going strong. Every year we take her out at least once, usually two or three times: the San Miguel River, the Green, the Dolores, the mighty San Juan.

The San Juan's The One: the lower gorge that leads from Mexican Hat to Clay Hills Crossing, across the Xanadus of southern Utah. That's the one you have to do, every year, to keep things together. Why? I don't know, it just is . . . the Ultimate River.

This particular year we had applied for a spring permit but were turned down. So we waited till the dead heat of midsummer, when the river is almost always empty, and called the BLM office over in Blanding. Sure enough, now we could have a permit, for as long as we wanted. The water was low, and the weather was hot, and there was nobody out there, just Mad Dogs and Englishmen, Mad Coyotes and Hard-Core River Rats.

We packed up the rafting gear, along with enough food for eight days and several ten-gallon water jugs. The San Juan in summer is barely liquid, a thick, opaque gravy of ground-up stone, mud, sand, with just enough H_2O to keep it from setting up into mortar: "Too thick to drink, too thin to plow," as the old-timers used to say. It quickly fouls any water filter you try to use on it.

Driving out, we got a taste of the weather we were going to endure. As we came down out of the mountains south of Lizard Head Pass, the temperature skyrocketed. Cortez, where we stopped for groceries, felt like Arabia, pedestrians drifting around in slow motion in the stunning heat, vehicles with their windows rolled up tight and air conditioners going full blast. Tongues of sand were creeping across the blacktop on the back road north of Sleeping Ute Mountain, and we were rocked by searing gusts of wind.

Bluff, where the road intersects the river, baked in its sand-stone canyon. The guy who sold us gas moved like molasses and could barely push the words out from between his lips: "Yep, shore is hot. Hadn't rained but once in three months, and when it did it just hit the ground and disappeared. Went up in smoke."

The last few miles down to the Hat were Highway 61 Revisited; we half expected to see prophets howling out in the badlands, anchorites ululating atop the crazy turrets of Valley of the Gods. Even in the AC interior of the Ford, it felt hot. I slugged down a whole six pack of Diet Cokes, my drink of choice, between Cortez and our first glimpse of Mexican Hat Rock, and I was still thirsty.

At the put-in, on the beach, we couldn't wait to leave. We virtually threw the dry bags, coolers, and water containers on board, made a desultory effort to tie them down, and then I drove the car back up to the Trading Post for the shuttle driver to deliver at Clay Hills. At the last second I bought two more six packs of soda and another tube of sunblock. Then I walked back down across the sunburnt desert, back down to the river. Nancy was already set to go, sitting in the bow. I filled my cap with river water, dumped it over my head, pushed us off the shore, and jumped in. Three minutes later the water had evaporated, and my cap and skull were again as dry as the proverbial bone.

It wasn't only hot, it was slow, slow going. The river was down to about 600 cubic feet per second, and the current barely moved. When we stopped paddling, an up-canyon wind promptly rose and tried its damnedest to blow us back the way we had come. When the San Juan is really running, 3,000 or 6,000 cfs or maybe even thrice that, the river does most of the work. You paddle to stay in the heart of the current, and to steer, and not much else. This trip, we were going to have to propel our

147

overloaded raft ourselves, oar stroke by oar stroke, the whole way. It already felt like a tough proposition.

But it was too late to turn back now. We scraped and banged our way over and through Gypsum Creek Rapid, and then passed under the highway bridge, carrying travelers south into Monument Valley and north toward Bluff, the Needles, Moab. A couple of hours later, we entered the gates of the main canyon. The cliffs closed in on both sides. Except for a few rough, very rough, foot trails, Honacker, Slickhorn, Grand Gulch, there was no way out for the next fifty-seven miles.

Our campsite the first night, a fine sand beach a mile or two into the gorge, at the very beginning of the Goosenecks, was immaculate. The only signs of life were the tracks of mice, small deer, and big birds. No human spoor at all. It was the classic trade-off: when conditions are less than ideal, you have a place to yourself. Nine times out of ten, it was a good deal. This, I thought, might be that tenth time, the exception that proves the rule.

The next day was hotter than ever. The river had dropped two or three inches from the night before, and as the day went on, the current seemed to curl up and die completely. *Requiescat in pace.*

We drifted on through the Goosenecks, those deeply entrenched meanders where the San Juan coils back on itself again and again, like a nautilus shell or a lariat. We were barely moving, going so slow we gave up looking at the river map and just kept paddling on, paddling on.

It was beautiful, but it was also kind of maddening; especially when a gust of wind came up on our bow and stopped us dead in the water, pushing us back till we fetched up on one bank or the other. Then we had no choice but to paddle like lunatics till we started almost imperceptibly moving again. It really took it out of you, both physically and psychologically.

By evening, we felt like we were paddling an iron barge up a river of mucilage. That night we drank like camels, gallons and gallons of water, tea, soda, and instant lemonade. There were white hieroglyphics of salt on our tanned, burned arms. Looking at the map, we couldn't figure out where we were, except that we were going nowhere fast and we still had a long, long way to go.

The next day was like the rest, only, yes, slower and hotter. At the rate we were going, we were never going to reach the takeout at Clay Hills on time. According to our trading post contract, we were supposed to pay the shuttle driver ten dollars an hour for waiting past the arranged pickup time. Meanwhile, how in the name of the Hero Twins was he, or she, supposed to survive for two days at the mosquito-ridden chaparral sump that was Clay Hills Crossing?

"If we don't start making up time, we can't afford to show up at Clay Hills," I joked. "I'll have to just give the driver the car to break even."

It actually was pretty funny, we decided. What was the big hurry, anyway? There were worse things than being behind schedule in Paradise. The moment we got home, we were just going to wish we were back out here again. That was the trap we human beings fidgeted our way into, over and over again. We were so busy looking where we were going and thinking about where we had been that meanwhile we were nowhere at all.

Fool's Gold

We passed the Honaker Trail that day and paddled on into the dusk before finally making camp . . . somewhere. Another fantastic beach, deep in the pre-Cretaceous sandstone gullet of Utah.

A great blue heron flew away down the canyon and vanished.

Six miles high above us, a big commercial jet rolled across the stratosphere in absolute silence, unreeling snow-white contrails behind that slowly broke apart and dissolved into blue-black space. Up there, in First Class, the grand imperial sachems of our age bapped away on their laptops, read Sun Tzu on war, flirted with the flight attendants, and drank themselves stuporous. They owned everything, as far as their eyes could see and beyond. Arctic oil leases, submarine nickel nodule mines, invisible trade routes across the skies; the Force That Through the Green Fuse Drives the Flower, the mineral rights to the very beach on which we camped. It was all dreams, of course, but if you dared say so, you were branded a terrorist, an outlaw, to be hunted down and killed. That's how it seemed, from the vantage point of that lonely, nameless beach on that wild river.

We continued on down the river, deeper and deeper into the strangely eroded layers of rock. High above, along the rims, the Cedar Mesa sandstone formed itself into Antonio Gaudí concert halls, cowboy hats, birds, ruined cathedrals out of Caspar David Friedrich paintings.

We ran Government Rapid, a tricky little ride down through too shallow water and lurking rocks, and camped on the beach just below. The middle of Nowhere, if Nowhere had a middle.

Consider this. If you managed to find a way up the little canyon that fissures its way back into the cliffs behind our camp—doubtful, but who knows? And if you found a way up the hundreds of feet of vertical sandstone behind that. And then if you managed to scramble up the next zone, of precariously sloping slickrock, and boulders and teetering talus cones, without dying of sunstroke, or rolling a rock and getting a greenstick tibial fracture, or blowing a kneecap. And then if you found a break in the skyscraper-tall rimrock up above, a fissure, a runoff, a crumbled ledge (breaks in the rimrock do exist, but they're as rare as sage hen's teeth).

Well, if you got that far, you'd have to be strong, sure footed, and above all lucky beyond the realm of the reasonable. And you would also be standing in deep Dreck, to say the least. See, you'd be standing in a maze of undulating waterless sandstone slickrock, where everything looks the same and route finding, well, route finding is impossible, because (a) there are no routes, and (b), you can't find them anyway.

And remember that other qualifier, waterless. That's the sinister part of these mesa tops, see. You might, just might, find a pool of old rainwater cupped somewhere in the slickrock, covered with green scum, with the corpse of a tarantula floating in it . . . if you're the Luckiest Person in the World, and you've been saying your prayers every night. But even if you do, what then? Unless you carried an empty Camelback out of the canyon with you (most unlikely), you can't take the water with you. No, all you can do is hydrate hydrate hydrate, till the pool is gone, and then start walking again, away from the rim. And remember, once you're through the rimrock, you'll be hiking in the loose sand and brush of the mesa, where the going is slow, navigation is hopeless, and there's no water at all, not a drop.

And you're still who knows how far from the nearest salvation, Navajo hogan, trading post, stock tank, sheep camp, whatever. There may not be another human soul (chinde, ghosts of the Navajo dead, don't count) for twenty-plus miles, two days—if you can find them.

I know; I've been there. In this same country, just north of the river, around Slickhorn and Lookout canyons. I had the advantage of one of the easiest routes, no, make that the easiest route by far, out of the inner gorge, and I still very nearly didn't make it. In fact, if it hadn't been for the pure-luck discovery of an old rusty trough, filled to the brim with icy spring water dripping from a sandstone ledge, I'd probably be a long-gone goner now—a grinning skull, a mummified pair of tennies, an expired Colorado driver's license in a bone fist.

No, pilgrim, this is remote, down here. Be humble, be very, very humble, in this awesome, awful country.

The next day we run the rapid at the mouth of Slickhorn. There's the old road coming down, built by the maniac wildcatter E. L. Goodridge, and along with it, Goodridge's wrecked equipment. Herein lies a tale, that's actually pretty funny (if you're not in the Oil Bidness). I quote from Miser (1922):

> The road was constructed many years ago by E. L. Goodridge for the purpose of lowering drilling machinery

to the bottom of the canyon, where there are large oil seeps. An engine, after being brought across the desert for a distance of more than 175 miles (taking 30 days to haul by mule from Gallup, New Mexico) was safely taken down the canyon wall to a point within a stone's throw of the drilling site, but at that point, due to an unfortunate accident, the engine tumbled from the road and over the cliffs to the bottom of the canyon and was thus broken beyond repair.

The true story of the Old West, the Iron Age, and Manifest Destiny in a nutshell: "One small step for man—one Giant Leap for—#@$%&*!!"

Goodridge, bless him, also built the first highway bridge at Mexican Hat, connecting Monument Valley with southeastern Utah. Alas, a flash flood carried that first bridge away a few years later. Let's hear it for Goodridge, Minor League Ozymandias of the Four Corners, Minister of Mining and Transportation for the Void and Emperor of Dreams!

We're at Grand Gulch by noon, and we're due to be at Clay Hills tomorrow, at noon. Looking at the map, there's no way we're going to make it. The current has totally died now: the river's surface looks like a sheet of dirty brown plastic, coated with dust motes, bits of wood, leaves. And we have fourteen miles to go.

Once more into the breach, dear fools, once more . . .

We start out paddling, but then the river ebbs into shallows around Trumbull Wash, sandbars and mud flats, and absolutely stops. We collapse on our paddles.

"I can't paddle another stroke," Nancy croaks. "I'm sorry, but I just can't." The poor girl is covered with sand, her clothes dun with soil and mud, blisters on her fingers. The smile she assembles on her face is so sad that I have to look away. She's been a trooper, but enough is enough.

It's time for another mode of propulsion. I climb down into the waist-deep water, grab the bow rope, and start walking. Yes, very much like Humphrey Bogart in *The African Queen.* Nancy sits in the stern beneath an old parasol and reads a book.

The canyon walls look twice as high when you are walking, not floating. The sun plays tabla riffs on my head. The light is hallucinatory: it dissolves the world, not into a Green thought in a green shade but a White hot incoherence in a blast furnace. But at least we're moving again, however slowly.

As the long afternoon drags on, I trudge down canyon. Occasionally, we hit a stretch of deep water where there's an actual strand of living, palpitating current. When we do, I use my life jacket to float me at the end of the rope and I freeload along, the raft and I in eccentric orbit, drifting around, along.

A beaver looks at me from a tamarisk thicket on the shore, does a double take, and then slips into the river and vanishes. A minute later he reappears, a few feet away, bright eyes checking me out.

I had a friend back in Virginia, one of the extreme kayakers who run the rapids at Great Falls on the Potomac, who claimed to have invented a new sport: he donned a bicycle helmet, snorkle, mask, and fins, and ran some of the small, fast rivers in the Southeast, swimming and floating. Of course, two or three people, beginning with the legendary white water guide Georgie Clarke, had already added neoprene wet suits to their equipage and swam and floated the Grand Canyon of the Colorado . . . much bigger rapids, but then they didn't have to share the river with cottonmouth moccasins and other ill-tempered Dixie serpents.

If you hit the San Juan during one of the months when it is comparatively clear, you could do the same thing here. I can't help thinking that it would be a great experience: seeing the river from the bottom up, drifting with the beavers, the giant catfish (the Navajos claim some are as big as a man), the squawfish and minnows . . .

Unfortunately, most of my voyages today don't last more than five or ten minutes. Then the current or the depth runs out, and I'm back to walking, dragging the raft along. By evening, Oljeto Wash is in sight. We should go farther, but I'm totally finished. My eyes are red and sore, my legs feel like empty parcels, my fingers sting where the rope rubbed them raw and the salts of sweat invade the flesh.

The last hour I'm purely on automatic pilot. I sing songs to myself to keep going, songs with a maritime air: "Yellow Submarine," "The Edmund Fitzgerald," "Sloop John B," "The Silkie Ballad," with rude desert lyrics improvised and interpolated with the originals. The last couple of hundred yards seem to last forever . . . till finally I squelch up onto the shore, Nancy clambers out, and we haul the raft up onto the dusty stony ugly little beach.

At high water, Oljeto is a marvelous place to camp. The lagoon laps up against a sandstone overhang; you can scramble up around the sides and set up your tent on the alluvial sandbars just above the dropoff. There are pools, shade, and a lovely view back out onto the main canyon and the river flowing. But at low water, and if this was much lower, it wouldn't be water, Oljeto is inaccessible. You're reduced to scraping out a tent site on the scrubby ledges up against the cliffs at the downriver end of the canyon mouth.

We're out of all the good food: the Thai noodles, the bagels and cream cheese, the cookies, the oranges, the tuna, salmon, gorp, granola, and tofu. The last Diet Coke vanished three days ago.

Dinner is crackers, bread the consistency of leather, rubbery cheese, peanut butter, granola bars that were bad new and have gone downhill from there, raw carrots, and coffee. All of our clothes are permeated with river mud. Our hair is full of sand.

We look at the map: eight miles to go. And we've been averaging maybe a mile an hour, on this Sea of Tranquillity with its paradoxically untranquil up-canyon winds.

Impossible.

The next morning, something of a miracle occurs.

There is always a jolt of current first thing in the day. I don't know why: something about the cool air, the cool rock, swifter masses of water from far upstream finally reaching these canyon fastnesses. Usually, the acceleration isn't that great, and it dies out after an hour or two. But this morning, when we push out into the river, it's fairly scooting along. Must be two miles an hour, maybe a hair more, and no upstream winds at all. We start paddling.

Steer Gulch and Whirlwind Draw fairly fly by (the sensation of speed is subjective, of course), and before we know it we're sashaying down the four-mile straightaway that leads to Clay Hills.

The canyon walls begin to drop away; the landscape unfolds like one of those paper flowers you drop into water. There are the Clay Hills, the Red Cliffs, distant mesas with forested sides and lofty white sandstone summits. The sky is suddenly huge, the vistas limitless. A hundred miles away, a pile of cumulus clouds as nacreous as mother-of-pearl cruises the horizon.

We haven't seen another human being in nine days. The San Juan Canyon has been our entire world, and the two of us the whole human race. Now, when we see the Navajo shuttle driver standing on the riverbank, a kid in orange, pink, green, blue, and yellow Fauvist pants from Wal-Mart and a long-sleeved Metallica T-shirt, raising his hand in solemn greeting, he looks like the Brother from Another Planet, an emissary from a Lost Continent. . . . And we, we probably look like a couple of Mudmen, the misshapen primordial monster-clowns the Pueblo and Navajo Indians believe inhabit these desert rivers, squeezed out of the mud, the rocks and sand and sent up into the daylight world of Men to do mischief and frighten the unwary.

But a trip's not over until it's over.

We had cleverly planned to rest up in Bluff on our way home, and with that in mind we had made a reservation at a motel for our first night out. We dropped the driver off in Mexican Hat, tipped him a ten, and drove north to Bluff. Only to learn that the ancient lady who owned the place had forgotten all about our reservation. She was full up, and so was every other motel in town, and ditto as far north as Blanding and Monticello. This was the peak of the summer season, when tourists from all over the world, Europe, Japan, you name it, tour the Canyonlands country in rental cars and tour busses with onboard guides. Every possible room is booked up months in advance.

The prospect of camping out one more night was unthinkable. We were hot, dirty, scratchy, itchy, exhausted, and uncomfortable. So we started driving homeward, hoping another miracle would happen along the way: a motel room. But the cosmos was plumb out of miracles, it turned out.

It was already evening, as we left Bluff and took the back roads north by east. The two-lane blacktop wobbled in my sun-addled vision. I don't remember much about the journey, except that Nancy was unconscious most of the way to Cortez. Where it was hot, and night, and NO VACANCY signs were everywhere.

Much of the rest of the traffic consisted of tourists in vans, RVs, Winnebagos, obviously in the same fix we were in; every time they reached a motel they slowed, looked, and then accelerated away again when they saw there was no room.

There was nothing for it but to go home. We took the long lone road up through Dolores, Stoner, Rico, passing maybe three or four other cars the whole way. Finally, at last, over Lizard Head Pass, by Trout Lake, with the first staticky signal from KOTO coming through on the radio. By the Ophir turn, and up again, over Turkey Creek Mesa; and down again, to Telluride, with all the familiar mountains looking down. . . . And then the last fifteen minutes to our house.

Driving that night, we found that we now understood perfectly the idea behind the phenomenon of pilgrimage. The physical journey to a sacred site, a geographic lodestone of compelling power, whether it be Mecca, Mt. Kailash, the Little Colorado River, Sipapu, Lourdes, Rome, Graceland. On our trek, like those, we were drawn irresistibly onward through bone weariness, night blindness, detours, wrong turns and false summits, disappointments, missed appointments and fickle circumstances, dry waterholes and abandoned caravanaries, till you finally arrive. At the canyon. At the Government Rapids beach. At Clay Hills Crossing . . . and then, home, at last.

We lived down valley back then, in a strange little earth house in Fall Creek with a deck overhanging the San Miguel River. It had its imperfections—radon, a dodgy toilet system hooked up to a minuscule septic tank, wood rats in the walls, and the constant drone of traffic passing almost overhead from Highway 145 less than three feet from the bedroom ceiling—but when we pulled in, down the dirt driveway through the tunnel of green branches and brush to the front door, it seemed like the original House Made of Dawn, the home built by the gods for the first men at the dawn of time.

First we took showers, washing away several ounces of geology and topography. Then we changed into clean clothes. Dry wool sox, baggy pants, pristine T-shirts and turtlenecks. I scraped a week and a half of bristly stubble from my chin. Then, it must have been midnight, we broached the supplies we'd picked up on our way through Cortez: sodas, juice, cold fried chicken, Grapenuts. And then we went to bed, and slept and slept and slept. . . . And the shiny black piano roll of the San Juan played in my sleep, a wild and jongling gamelan, all night long.

Why haven't I lived my whole life this authentically, with such strength, determination, and intensity? Anything else is a waste of time, and time, after all, is all we've got. Especially here in the mountains, where we are constantly reminded of the glories of eternity all around us: you'd think we'd learn. Clean out our lives, get rid of everything false and bogus, dumb and dull, counter-feit and snide, and live the way we know we can but keep for-getting . . .

The river is waiting for us; it's been waiting for millions of years, to carry us away.

The Last Jew in Oiltown

A couple of years after I moved down to Telluride, the town's small but growing Jewish population decided to celebrate the Seder at the Senate Bar. I didn't go—I think I was camped out that night up on Deep Creek Mesa, attempting to do a Native American vision quest—but the event ended up as one of the real bellwether happenings in modern Telluride history.

See, Everett Murrell was the town marshal back then, and Everett was, well, not exactly at home in the late twentieth century. A sawed-off, red-faced runt of a man who wore six-shooters and boasted of his "quick draw," he resembled more than anything Barney Fife's twisted and malign twin brother. He hated the newcomers (like me) who were flocking to Telluride, opening up stores and businesses and running for political office.

His hate took strange, paranoia-warped forms. For instance, he decided that my attorney, weisenheimer Bob Korn, was a big-time drug kingpin. Reason? Korn was from New York City; Korn liked to listen to Dylan with the sound cranked up all the way at his big house on the Sunnyside of town. Ah, but the crux clue was, Korn kept his attic window open!

Now, Korn left said window open for typical Kornsian reasons: he was sorting through stuff up there one summer, and it was stiflingly hot and he wanted some fresh air. And then he left it open for the next couple of years because he was too damn lazy to climb back up there and close it. But in the rank abyss of Murrell's mind, the window was open because Korn was venting fumes from an illegal drug lab! So Everett and one or another of his australopithecine deputies spent hours every day parked down the hill from Korn's house, running surveillance on the "operation." Everett and company never announced publicly just what kind of drug Korn was producing in his attic, whether it was merry-jew-wanna, heroin, black beauties, or yellow jackets. Truth was, the Everett Crime Force didn't know too much about drugs. I remember when they arrested a local for possession of something like eleven peyote cactus buttons, and one of the deputies went on the radio to enlighten the public. His spiel went something like this: "Peyote is a mushroom. It can be smoked, snorted, or injected by its users, who sometimes refer to it as 'Miggles' or 'Skank.' A single button sells on the street for as much as a thousand dollars."

Now, I'm not accusing Everett and company of anti-Semitism or anything like that—I mean, who knows what really goes on in the hollow sanctum sanctorum of a policeman's mind?—but on the night of the Seder, Murrell and his deputies, guns drawn, came crashing into the Senate yelling that everyone had to go home or face immediate arrest. The charge: serving liquor without a permit!

Alas, Everett had read the tea leaves of the future cockeyed and completely wrong. The town of Telluride, and not just the Jews, sent the marshal packing, posthaste. When you are trying to establish your town as a "year-round mountain resort," loose screwballs like Everett just don't fit in. The last thing you want is a story in the *New York Times* Travel Section with the head "JEWS NOT WELCOME IN COLORADO'S NEWEST RESORT."

Nope.

Besides, as any literate westerner could have told Everett, the Wild, Wild West has always been full of Wild, Wild Jews. What would the cowboys and forty-niners have done without Levis? Is Barry Goldwater "western" enough for yuh, pilgrim? Some of the biggest cattle ranches on the plains were owned and operated by tough German Jews right off the boat. "Da bunkhouse ist ungeposht, boys, let's clean her up!" I remember seeing an old photograph in a packinghouse office in the Midwest, of a tiny barrel-chested character in a ten-gallon hat, yee-hawing triumphantly atop a huge "unrideable" bronco while a mob of cowpokes, gunsels, and saddle tramps cheered wildly. The man's name was something like Isaac Rosenberg, and he owned half of central Montana back in the 1890s.

The San Juans were no different. Otto Mears, who built the roads that opened up these near impassable mountains and chasms, hacking and dynamiting impossible roads out of vertical rock and thin air, was called "The Hebrew Pathfinder of the San Juans."

Anyhow, we're all strangers out this away, aren't we? Except for the Utes and the Navajos, we Americans, westerners, southern Rocky Mountain émigrés, we're all a bunch of Wandering Jews, a tribe of lost souls exiled in the Vastness, searching for home . . . ours, or somebody else's.

Southwest of the San Juans, in northern New Mexico, is an area that would fit right in in the direst parts of Texas, Oklahoma, and Louisiana. They drill for oil down there, and the towns, Aztec, Farmington, Bloomfield, and the rest, are populated largely by bony, barracuda-faced Elvises in pickup trucks whose stickers brag, "OIL FIELD TRASH & PROUD OF IT!" warn "U.S. OUT OF RED U.N.," and fly the Stars and Bars of the Confederacy unabashedly. Gun shows, pawnshops, and meth labs are big time.

I had flown down to Farmington from Telluride on some kind of monkey business, taken a cab over to Oilton for a meeting, and got a ride back to the airport with the same taxi. My driver was a hard-faced, wild-haired, young guy, a typical local (I thought). We were crawling through the endless traffic lights, talking about the usual, politics and sports, when the driver volunteered, "Ya know, I guess I'm jest about the last Je-e-ew in Oilton."

I was nonplussed. "Uh, really?"

"Yep." He paused to dip a wad of snuff. "See, my mother's from Noo York. She was always kinda wild, I guess, and when she met muh dad she drapt outa college and married him and moved out here. Her parents couldn't believe it, they didn't know whether to piss or go blind—a nice Jewish girl, father a doctor, marryin' a goddam West Texas roustabout." He grinned.

"So you grew up here?"

"My brother and me, we were born right here in Oilton. Same crummy trailer my ma's still livin' in. My dad wasn't worth a shit. He took off when I was a year old. Good riddance."

We passed a company pickup truck with three oil field workers jammed in the cab. The driver raised a hand to them in greeting, and all three returned the greeting.

"How was it?"

"Growin' up here? It wan'nt bad. My brother, he's two years older, was on the wrasslin' team, and I played football. We were pretty popular, guess you'd say. Couple of good ol' boys from Midland-Odessa moved here, they tried givin' us shit one time about bein' Jee-ews, but after my brother kicked their asses all the way inta the hospital, that kinda put an end to it."

"I bet. Your brother still around?"

Shook his head. "Joined the Navy right outa high school to get in the Seals. He's stationed in Portsmouth, Virginia."

"So there's just you left?"

"Well, my mother's still here, but a few years ago she decided she didn't want to be a Jew no more. Got inta one of those New Age churches or whatever they call 'em. Changed her name ta some Hindoo thing, Pandoorasawamy, some nonsense like that. I told her, yer kiddin' yerself, Mom. Once a Jew, always a Jew. Ya can't change it."

"Is it, ah, lonely? Being the only one left?"

He grinned again, and shook his head. "It's the opposite a lonely, if anything. I know who I am, see. That's all that matters. Sometimes I think someday I'll get on a plane, and fly on over to Is-ra-el, and look around. I'll go to that Wailin' Wall they got there, an' say, 'Howdy there, and shalom. This is Dwayne Austin, from Oilton, New Mexico. My mom's name's Kaplan, Andrea Kaplan. How y'all doin', here in the Holy Land?'"

Tall Tales

A bunch of locals were sitting around the Elks Club on one of those stormy spring nights, when the wet snow just won't stop pounding down, and the wind blows first one way down Colorado Avenue, then the other. Mud Season, some call it; others, Dead Season. The whole town seems deserted, abandoned. It's a good time of year to recollect the great deeds and follies of the past and spin them into yarns.

Tall tales really are an art form. The best of them contain enough truth to sound almost feasible; they play off the natural surreality of the West, its scale and its eccentricity. Mountain Man Jim Bridger parlayed the petrified logs of Wyoming into whole forests of petrified trees, with petrified birds in the petrified branches singing petrified songs. A mountain of volcanic glass, obsidian, became a clear glass mountain that operated like a huge spyglass: looking through it, you could see a thousand miles. And it was so clear that the Shoshone Indians used to deliberately chase buffalo herds toward it; the bison ran headlong into the glass cliffs, knocking themselves cold.

I wonder if Bridger's fable inspired F. Scott Fitzgerald's story, "The Diamond as Big as the Ritz"?

"Did I ever tell you about the Wood Rat?" asked Jeff Campbell. Campbell was an intense-looking, adrenalized little guy, one of the founders of the Telluride Ski Patrol and a pioneer hang glider pilot.

There was a chorus of negatives.

"It happened last year. I started finding things chewed up around the house—old boots and sweaters, skis, ski wax, snowshoes, camping gear. My wife and I thought it was the kids, playing tricks on us, but they swore up and down it wasn't them. Then we started finding giant piles of rodent shit here and there, pellets the size of gumdrops, and we knew we had a Wood Rat in the house.

"I got a flashlight and crawled under the house, and I caught sight of him—he was huge! So I went down to Montrose and bought myself a great big hair-trigger trap at Country General. I took it under the house and baited it with a couple of ounces of rotten cheese. I figured that was that.

"When I went back down there the next morning, the cheese was gone but the trap hadn't gone off. Those Wood Rats are smart! So I set up the trap again, and this time I got me some

Cheez Whiz and smeared it all over the base of the trap. OK, I thought, that'll get the bastard. But when I came down the next morning, the critter'd cleaned every bit of Cheez Whiz off the trap, left it clean as a whistle, without setting it off.

"I got kind of paranoid at that point. For a while I thought my wife was doing it, working with the Wood Rat to drive me crazy. Then I thought maybe my old ski patrol friends were coming up from town and setting the traps off before the Wood Rat got there. But then I thought, Nope, they weren't smart enough to pull something like that, and besides they were too damned lazy. It had to be the Wood Rat, working on his own.

"So I went back down to Country General and bought two more traps. I took all three of them down under the house and rigged them up in a triangle, so there was no way of getting into one without one of the others going off. I baited them with the Cheez Whiz again, and this time I put a layer of sticky peanut butter over everything, so you'd get caught up in that getting to the cheese. It was foolproof, like the kind of trap Einstein would have come up with if he had Wood Rats in Princeton, New Jersey.

"Anyhow, the next morning I went down there. I took my Polaroid, with a flash, to take a picture of the dead Wood Rat."

He paused dramatically.

"What happened, Campbell?"

"This time the Wood Rat had eaten everything, and then somehow set off all three traps without getting caught in them. And he'd hauled one of my good Bean boots down from the mud room, ate a bunch of holes in that, and left it there, like a Declaration of War. Like, You want to screw with ME? Hey, I'll screw with YOU!"

"So what did you do?"

Campbell shrugged. "What could I do? I gave up. I threw the traps away and declared a unilateral cease-fire."

"Did it work?"

"Well, the rat's still there, but now we treat him kind of like a household pet. We put food and water out for him, and he doesn't steal as much as he used to. We call him Ratzilla."

"I've got a much, much worse story," a guy named Howdy piped up. "A Skunk Story."

"Aww, everybody up here's got a Skunk Story," someone scoffed.

"Not like this one, man. This Skunk destroyed my whole life. Seriously."

"Destroyed your life? Right," the Unbeliever said.

"I'd just moved here, back in the seventies. My wife and I were just out of college, Dartmouth for me, Holyoke for her. We had a nest egg from our parents, about $90,000, and we figured we could make our fortune here in one big deal."

"$90,000? That's not a nest egg, it's a goddam omelette," a wise guy laughed.

"I borrowed another $45,000, and got an option on a couple of pieces of land around here," Howdy went on. "Ten percent down. Remember, this was back when land was still cheap. Then we put together a development plan and sent it off to a dozen friends of the family who had money to invest. We invited them to come down and check the place out.

"We put on a big feed the first night they all got here. We had it catered—elk meat, prime rib, oysters, champagne. It cost a fortune, but remember, we figured we were going to bring in $1.5 million that week, and with the land in hand we'd turn that into a good ten million in five years.

"We were renting this big house we couldn't afford, where the kitchen kind of segued into a huge dining room. Everyone was mingling, when all at once the cat door opened in the kitchen and in marched this black-and-white tomcat and started eating the cat food by the door. Now, my wife had a cat back then, but it wasn't black and white, it was one of those poofy, purple-colored Maine cats, name of Mookie. But I didn't notice; I was too busy talking it up with the guests, easements and up-zoning and water rights and year-round recreation, and all the money we were all going to make—

"When suddenly one of the guests, the wife of some investment banker from New York, saw the strange feline at the cat dish, and recognized what it was. Not only recognized it but let out a scream that could wake the dead. 'OHMIGOD, IT'S A SKUNK!!!'

"Well, everyone bolted like it was a Bengal tiger at the cat dish instead of a sixteen-ounce polecat. These were city people from Back East, remember. Yelling, screeching, cussing.

"Everything still could have been fine. I grabbed a slice of prime rib and put on my best airline pilot–type voice, 'Nothing to worry about, folks. It's just a tiny little skunk, that's all, heh heh heh, as long as we don't spook him,' and I walked real slowly and quietly across the kitchen. My plan was to open the kitchen door and then toss twenty-five bucks' worth of Kansas City beef outside, and when the skunk took off after it I'd close the door after him and then nail the goddam cat door shut.

"But I reckoned without Mookie. Or maybe it was the Ute Curse everyone talks about, who knows? Just when I got to the key point where the skunk, the kitchen door, and I formed an isosceles triangle about three feet on a side, the skunk watching me while he kept on eating, my wife's damned feline comes through the goddam cat door, and sees the skunk eating her food. Mookie leaps at the skunk, who immediately executes a ninja 180 and sprays both her and me, a direct hit, and then takes off like a rocket, still spraying, up across the counters of food and through the panicking guests, pursued by %$#@*ing Mookie, flying blind but in hot pursuit—

"Sometime in the midst of it all, my wife, who always had the gift for saying exactly the wrong thing at the wrong time, she started laughing hysterically and she said to me, really loudly, 'MY HUSBAND, THE GREAT SKUNK HUNTER! THE REAL ESTATE KING OF THE SAN JUANS!'

"Well. I guess at that point I threw the Skunk Bait prime rib at her. Unfortunately, I hit her. Which led to one of the weirdest spousal abuse cases southern Colorado's ever seen—"

"It's true!" Campbell hooted. "And then she sued his sorry ass in civil court—"

"The end result?" Howdy said. "No land deal. Lost the option money. Six months' work release in Montrose—"

"The old Grey Bar Hotel," someone commented. "Been there, done that."

"Who hasn't?" came another glum comment.

"I lost everything," Howdy said.

"Hey, except for your job on the Ski Patrol, don't forget about that," Campbell interjected.

"Yeah, I guess you're right. The skunk didn't so much ruin my life as turn it around."

"Yeah, if you'd pulled off that land deal, you'd probably weigh three hundred pounds by now and be just another fat bastard with a real estate office on Main Street."

"A trophy wife with a boob job, who hates your guts."

"Chill out on the skunk. You should find him and kiss his black-and-white ass. He saved your life. And that's the truth."

"They don't make 'em like they used to," growled a voice from the rear. "And that includes the lot of you."

There was a muffled chorus of laughter and rebuke from the room.

"Ralph, you're so damned old you used to sit God on your knee and scold him—'Cut out these goddam avalanches'—Oh, excuse me."

Ralph laughed his dry cackling laugh. "Back in the fifties, that was when Telluride was Telluride." Ralph had been the town's only lawman back then, when prostitution, gambling, and bootlegging complemented the town's mining economy.

"Tell 'em about the Hodunk kid!" another ancient yelled.

"That little bastard," Ralph rasped, as if it had only been yesterday. The Hodunk kid had probably succumbed to old age years ago. "He had one a the first cars in town, a souped-up

Chevrolet roadster, and he thought he was real smart. I'd start chasin' him for speeding, and he'd cut through alleys and back-yards, and finally he'd get away. I could catch him on the straight and level, but he'd lose me on the hills. And then the judge, they musta been related, he'd give him a week in the pokey and threaten to take his license away.

" 'Take his license away!' I'd yell. 'He lost his license two years ago!' And jail, that was just a week's vacation for him. Better than workin' in the mines.

"Finally, I arrested him, and instead of takin' him to jail, I drove him to his ma's house, where he lived.

" 'What're you doin'?' he asked.

" 'I'm takin' you to your ma.' She worked days cleaning rooms at the Sheridan and nights barkeeping at the old Roma, and she musta weighed in at two-fifty, and none of it fat.

" 'Hey, you don't have to do that!' All of a sudden he didn't look so damn smart!

"I woke up his ma and told her, 'I've been chasin' Junior here all over town for the best part of six hours.'

" 'Oh, yeah?' she said. 'Well, leave him here, an' I'll take care of it.'

"The next day I saw him, and he was all crimped up and black and blue—he could hardly walk. I smiled to him and said, 'How's tricks, Mister Hodunk?'

"He looked at me and said, 'You smart sonofabitch, I told ya to take me to jail. Now look what happened.'

"He never gave me any trouble after that."

It was a tough town back then, no doubt about it.

"When we come back from Korea, we were lookin' to raise hell, and we went down to Big Billie's. We got drunk, and Buckwheat started breakin' bottles on the bar. Big Billie's boyfriend of the moment was a little guy named Frenchie, from Canada, and when he told Buckwheat ta stop, Buckwheat just laughed at him. Well, he stopped laughing when Big Billie came barrelin' outa the back room hoisting a big meat cleaver. The rest of us made ourselves scarce, and Big Billie chased Buckwheat out of the bar and down the street while everyone laughed at him. 'Hail the Conquering Hero.' " Big Billie was Telluride's last madame, beloved and feared by all.

They were a hard bunch, back then. "I remember one Saturday night a miner named Johnson didn't like the way another miner was dancing with his wife, so he shot him. Then he chased the ambulance down valley, ran it off the road, and shot the guy again for good measure. Luckily, the guy survived.

"Johnson lit out for Grand Junction, but before we could arrest him a little Mexican gal stabbed him to death with a knife. I always felt bad about it, when they sent her to prison for it. They should've given her a medal. If ever a man needed killing, it was him."

I've got my own tall tale: only mine, of course, is 100 percent bona fide true, not like those other guys' fabulous constructions, God forgive them.

I was climbing a big peak north of Telluride, one of the highest in the state. Alone, as I frequently was those days. It was early summer, and there were still big snowfields splotched across the scree slopes. As the mountain began to dwindle away toward its summit, I found a set of tracks in the snow. Not human: few if any people had been up the peak yet that season. They were the tracks of a raccoon, a big one, and they were heading up, the same way I was. I followed them.

Snowfield to snowfield, I tracked the big 'coon up the mountain. His course was steady, straight toward the top, as if he too wanted to scrawl his name or leave his mitt print on the summit register. I kept expecting the tracks to turn away, to head back down—what is there to eat at 14,000 feet, after all?—but they never did.

I humped up the last snowfield, still tracking, till I reached the summit. And there, in the center of the snow, at the exact finite high point, the tracks ended in midstride, as if the raccoon had been plucked away into Heaven. Beyond was empty, trackless snow; and then the mountainside, plummeting away into emptiness.

There you go: as mysterious as, or even more than, Hemingway's frozen leopard high on Kilimanjaro. Did an eagle snatch the raccoon away? Unlikely: an adult raccoon is a burly fellow, well able to take care of her- or himself from aerial assault. And why did the raccoon climb to 14,250 feet and some anyhow? For the view?

Remember, Raccoon is co-Trickster with Coyote in Native American myth, wiser than man, fond of leaving false clues and playing tricks on his human cousins.

Anyhow, not a bad story, huh?

Running the Rockies

Wherever you live out here, there's a run out your front door. I can't imagine living in a place that doesn't have its own trail, one you don't have to drive to, and one where you're traveling on earth, not concrete or asphalt. That seems to me to be as necessary a part of life as a roof, running water, or heat in the winter. Maybe I've lived in the San Juans a little too long.

I have a house in Lawson Hill now, Telluride's "working-class" suburb, three-plus miles west of town at the very rim of the upper valley. If I run west, down valley, I follow the old railroad grade down into Ilium Valley. It's a fine route, with great views down into the deep gorge of the San Miguel, and a vast panorama of Sunshine Peak and the Wilsons as you turn the corner a mile or so down the trail. There are elk, coyotes, and occasionally black bears.

It does have its drawbacks. There are power lines overhead at the start of the trail, and a supremely ugly water tank off to the right. In the summer it's hot and dusty and often overpopulated with mountain bikers, who in my mind are but one short step above ATVers and off-road motorcyclists.

Anywhere else but here it would be choice; but I live here, not anywhere else.

Much better, the trail that has become an inseparable part of my everyday existence, is the trail up valley, into town. Not the paved trail along the Highway 145 spur, the other one: the River Trail, that winds along the base of pine-covered mountainsides, paralleling the San Miguel River, at the edge of the Valley Floor.

Hardly anyone runs it, for some reason, making it even sweeter. And it goes on and on, if you want it to and you've got the oomph. You can follow it all the way through Telluride and then turn up Bear Creek, or continue on up the road to the Pandora Mine and the waterfalls above and beyond. Other variations include the steep cutoff up Boomerang Road, or across and up to the Waterline Trail, and thence down to town.

I could take off at my door and end up communing with a mountain lion up on the Highline or glissading down a summer snowdrift atop Palmyra Peak's ridgeline, and never stop running the whole way.

So here's how it goes.

I start out on the gravel surface of my own block, San Miguel Ridge Road, hit the pavement for a couple of hundred feet, and then cut down on a dirt trail that runs below the main road, in the timber. Back up to the asphalt again, for maybe five minutes. Then I come to the highway, cross it onto grass and dirt, climb over the barbed-wire fence, and I'm on the River Trail. Which quickly climbs from cow pasture into forest.

The property I'm on is called the Valley Floor. It stretches all the way from the western edge of the town of Telluride three miles to the highway turnoff to Cortez. Back during the mining days it doubled as grazing land and a dumping ground for mine tailings, and the San Miguel has been channelized the whole length of it, dug into an arrow-straight artificial bed, leaving the old oxbows and curves as pools, gravel beds, wetlands. Now it's owned by one Neal Blue, an industrialist and investor from San Diego, whose professed plans for it include a resort hotel, artificial lakes, luxury homes, and, of course, a golf course. Doom and damnation. Luckily, the people of Telluride have unified to fight the development plan and annex the Valley Floor as Open Space, so I may get to do this run ten, twenty years from now, unmolested by security guards and the flying white spheroids of rotund businessmen in ridiculous clothes.

Anyhow, it's a perfect day. It's always a perfect day on this trail. Rain or shine, sleet or slush, perfect.

The trail wends its way through the woods, across lovely little meadows and back into the timber again. Water comes gushing down the steep side of Turkey Creek Mesa, boiling marble in the shadows of the big trees. In reality, this forest isn't that old—the miners totally logged off the whole Telluride area, to get wood

179

for mine timbers, fuel, building—but it feels, smells old. Its dark floor whispers of age-old secrets, buried there, that we may never find.

Tolstoy wrote, "I used to believe that there is a green stick, buried on the edge of a ravine in the old Zakaz forest at Yasnaya Polyana, on which words were carved that would destroy all the evil in the hearts of men and bring them everything good." I believe this same stick, or one like it, is hidden somewhere along the River Trail. Maybe some day, if I live long enough, I'll find it: unearthed by a spring black bear, hunting bugs and roots, or by a frost heave in an obscure meadowed glade.

I've run "seriously," the Pikes Peak Marathon, the 18½-mile Imogene Pass Run from Ouray to Telluride, the annual Ski Patrol Boomerang Road Race, but the runs like today's are the only ones that really count. No times, no goals, and no limits; HT&E, "here, there, and everywhere" runs, they call them in the Sierra Nevada. The course is in your heart, mirroring the forests, puddles, streams, bogs and stones, thickets and deadfall you find along your way. The trail ends where it always ends, where you started out: home.

Dancing in
Circular Time

One thing you learn up here: time is totally different. Our planet swims in an Age of Urbs, cities, metropolises, suburbs, sprawling Royal Nonesuches like "Los Angeles," "The Valley," the Beyond-the-Beltway expanses of northern Virginia. Most of us who moved to Telluride back in the seventies were city kids, veterans of that cold, denatured, quartz-clock world. We measured out our lives not in coffee spoons, but in rush hours, nine to fives, semesters, "breaks," synchronized traffic signals, and Sweeps Weeks . . . and sad "novelties" like Oscar Night, Derby Day, Super Bowl Sunday. . . . "And this year's winner IS—Hey, Mom, I'm going to Disneyland!"

Fool's Gold

"In the city every year is different, and they all add up to nothing," one old-time Telluride joker once said. Of course, we always laugh when we hear the truth.

Life in the mountains is quite another thing.

Every year is like another lifetime, a reincarnation of the last and progenitor of the next but at the same time unique unto itself. It's like I imagine the Dreamtime of the Australian Aborigines must be: time in a slow circle dance instead of a hundred-yard dash.

A true Mountain Calendar would contain entries like this (just a sampler):

—First aspens turn yellow.
—First sub-zero night (for all you kitchen gardeners).
—First snow on the peaks.
—Bears raid the dumpsters and then hole up.
—Chop firewood.
—Ski area opens.
—The Winter Solstice.
—The January Thaw.
—Mud Season.
—Hummingbirds return from the South.
—High Country opens up (enough snowpack melts off so normal human beings can hike to Navajo Lake, Silver Lake, etc.).
—Highline Trail opens.
—Fourth of July Parade and Fireworks. Rowdy rides his horse into the Sheridan Bar.

It's a pagan calendar, pagan year, tied to the eternal verities of sun, moon, slant of seasons, the blooming of wild plants, and the visitations of birds. What did this mean to us immigrant Telluridians? Well, almost without knowing it, we found ourselves living lives in tune with those eternal verities.

Sometimes, it was scary: after all, it was life and time without a safety net, without those distractions and anodynes the urban world offered. When you had time to stop and think about it. Maybe that helps account for the style of partying up here. Which has always been, well, extreme, if you will. Frenzied, perhaps. Compulsive. Driven. Dionysian. Mad.

So: Saturday night in Telluride. The Kamikaze Klones are playing at the Moon, or maybe it's Ralph Dinosaur and the Volcanoes, or String Cheese Incident, all bands with local roots of one kind or another. I'm dancing with the Buddhist nun with the implants, or the mountain-climbing divorcee from Aspen, or the Jack Mormon girl with the tattoo on her lower belly of a rose wrapped in barbed wire.

"It's easy to go crazy here; the trail is real well marked," as my friend Trumbull used to say.

A Rasta couple is dancing up a storm, dreads flying. The Rastas are an interesting phenomenon, white kids into extreme skiing and snowboarding, strong pot, and righteous (vegan) food. A few of them are well to do, leading to the nickname "Trustafarian" = Rasta + Trust Fund. They were once a major political and social force in Telluride, with a representative on the town council and their own thunkety-chunk Rasta band, "8750" (after the town's altitude). Still a presence here.

But that's neither here nor there. Crooked mine owners, crooked realtors; desperate dancing girls, hard-bodied husband-hunting face-liftees down from Aspen to check out the field; even those electrical genii the Pinheads have their incarnations, like Bryan Miller, who makes breathtaking furniture out of dis-assembled junked bicycles, right down to the spokes, chains, and inner tubes, and Joe Powell, inventor of the revolutionary Water-wolf line of rivercraft.

And someone's dealing black tar heroin to the young dragon chasers, they say, in the same alley where the Chinaman sold opium and morphine to broken-hearted good-time gals a hun-dred years ago, to sweeten their dreams and mend their wounded sleep . . .

No, nothing changes.

If sleek, sly Bulkeley Wells came waltzing through the room and swept little Miz Jack Mormon out the door into the night, or Rowdy Roudebush punched out Colonel Livermore of the mine owners' union-busting army, or the Sundance Kid stole the King of the Realtor's Beamer to make a crank run down to Nor-wood or Ridgway, I wouldn't be surprised.

That's circular time we're dancing to, podner, what goes around comes around and an allemande left on the ole left hand, and what goes around comes around, yippi-ki-yi-ay git along lit-tle dogies, till we all end up at closing time up at Lone Tree, the Marble Orchard, pushing up wild mountain grass in the wind and the moon, and no wonder we're all a little bit crazy, dancing so hard so long in this thin, hard air. Dancing till we drop.

Tenderfoot Blues

For the past decade we've seen the greedheads and fools pillage, plunder, and desecrate the mountains we live in like there's no tomorrow. They've drained ancient alpine bogs to build golf courses, bulldozed old-growth timber to make room for obscene trophy homes, hyped the real estate market so high that old-timers and working people alike have been forced to leave.

This is the dark side of democracy: that one Yahoo can destroy an entire valley, town, or ecosystem because he has the "right" to. Everyone has rights in America; only some people have bigger rights than others. Hey, they paid good money for them, didn't they?

But life goes on; and I mean that in the deeper sense. They won't kill off the San Juans that easily.

In a town near here, there lived a rich man who had moved west after making his fortune in outlet malls in the Midwest. Pakliotes by name, a large fat man with long gray hair and a tiny mustache. He bought himself a good-sized ranch abutting the town on one side, and announced to one and all that he was now a "cattleman." He erected an expensive stone and log gate at the entrance to his new spread, with a sign that read, in stylized letters seemingly scorched into the wood like a cattle brand, LONE EAGLE RANCH. He tore down the barbed-wire front fence and replaced it with a wooden pole fence, and then, when that looked too new, hired a crew of local ne'er-do-wells, crack-head cowpokes, and barstool bronco busters, and paid them $15 an hour to "distress" it with hammers till it looked like an authentic fence from the Melody Ranch or the Cartrights. He took to wearing enormous custom-made Stetsons and hand-tooled belts with personalized buckles, and he liked to drive around town in an antediluvian Ford pickup that looked and ran like perfect hell, so "real" it hurt.

He had bought the truck off old Two-Step McPhee his second week in town. Pakliotes saw it idling in front of the post office one day; he braked his Land Cruiser to a screeching halt in the middle of the street and hurried over to where Two-Step sat behind the wheel, going through his mail, bills, and G.I. disability checks, the truck running with a sound like a logging chain tossed into a cement mixer.

"How much'll you take for this truck?" Two-Step looked out at him through the cracked window. Make fun a ME, will you, ya goddam Eye-talian pencil dick?? To the innocent Two-Step, all humanity was either White American, Mexican, Knee-grow, Chinaman, Injun, or a catchall category, Eye-talian. "How much'll you pay me fer not gettin' outa my truck and kickin' yer smart ass?" Two-Step growled.

"I'm serious," Pakliotes protested, digging in his jacket pocket and coming up with his roll of "walk-around money," big enough to choke the Ophir Gopher, famous throughout the county back in the late forties for her prodigious oral talents.

"Well, I'll be dipped in shit," Two-Step muttered, as Pakliotes started peeling off the Benjamins. He got to fifty hundreds, then eighty, then a hundred. Two-Step had been offered $100 for his truck by the Naturita Junk Yard just last week. "It's only good for parts, and the parts ain't any good either," the smart ass'd grinned. Pakliotes kept counting.

Pakliotes kept counting till he ran out of hundreds, and the roll was gone. He held out the $11,300 in his big, soft hand. "We got a deal?"

Two-Step may have been a fool, but he was nobody's fool but his own. He could nearly smell the avarice, comin' off this here fat sonofabitch like smoke off a steak.

"Waal, the thing is, how'm I suppose to get around, if I sell ya my truck?" he whined querulously.

"How're you supposed to get around if you don't sell it?" Pakliotes laughed. "Smells like you already blew the head gasket. And that knock, sounds like you're going to need a valve job any day now." He leaned in the window, proffering the money insistently.

"Ten thousand more," old Two-Step said, meeting his gaze steadily.

"Twenty-five hundred more, and that's my last offer."

"Ten."

"Five."

"Ten."

"I'm not playing games here."

"Me neither. Ten."

In the end, Pakliotes wrote him out a check for the ten, on his account at the Mercantile Bank & Trust in Indianapolis, Indiana, bringing the total price to $21,300: enough, Two-Step figured, to buy himself one of them Toyota 4WDs secondhand, pay off his tab at the Hitching Post, get a new Remington at Wal-Mart before next elk season, and have enough left over to eschew work for a year or two. Then he drove Pakliotes even crazier by insisting they go together to the San Miguel Basin Bank across the street and cash the check there before he handed over the title.

"I just bought the old Packard Ranch," Pakliotes protested. "I'm good for it!"

"So what do I do if the check doesn't clear? Walk out to your ranch and have you pay me off in ten thousand dollars' worth of fresh bullshit?"

Pakliotes had to go along with it.

For the next few months Pakliotes was a happy man. When he wasn't back in the Midwest tending to his outlet mall deals, he was hanging out in Norwood, driving up and down Main Street in Two-Step's truck, feeling like the San Miguel County Kid. But in time, Pakliotes's mind began to turn, inevitably, toward money again.

Real Estate was booming up in Telluride, and the ripples spread all the way down to Montrose, Ridgway, Norwood. . . . Hell, a man'd have to be a fool not to take advantage of it! Pakliotes threw away his catalogs for mail-order bull jizm; tractors; pre-fab stables; and handmade Thunderbird silver, gold, turquoise, and petrified wood .357 Magnum revolver pistol grips, and hired himself a resort land planner. They went over the map of Lone Eagle Ranch, drawing in roads, houses, condominiums, an artificial lake.

They jotted out promo copy on a yellow legal pad, aided by a $350-an-hour ad whiz on the speaker phone out of San Francisco: "LONE EAGLE RANCH. BUY A PIECE OF THE DREAM. YOUR SECOND HOME IN THE WEST. LESS THAN 40 MINUTES FROM TELLURIDE. YEAR-ROUND 360-DEGREE SOLAR. HORSEBACK, TENNIS, GOLF. . . ." Then they took their plan to the mayor for approval, since two-thirds of the ranch lay within the eccentrically wide-ranging town limits.

The mayor was a sure thing, Pakliotes told himself. A conservative Republican named Buddy Gonzales, aged seventy but spry as a whiptail lizard, sporting an enormous dark beard that made him look (Pakliotes thought) like one of those Ayawhatchamacallums over in Iran, the mayor had a big blown-up photo of John Wayne on his office door, the Duke sneering as he pulled a six-shooter on whoever wanted to go inside. Gonzales insisted on flying the Gadsden flag, the one with the angry rattlesnake and the motto "Don't Tread On Me," just below the Stars and Stripes in front of Town Hall.

A week later Pakliotes put on his biggest Stetson and went back to Town Hall to pick up his rubber-stamped proposal. To his surprise, when he got there, Gonzales called him into the conference room, where the rest of the Town Board, Ethel Moody, Rex Royce, Marvella Sweet, and Martin Pollard, sat, deadpan as a bunch of poker-playing Navajos. The mayor sat himself down in the center. He placed Pakliotes's plans on the table, motioning for Pakliotes to take the lone empty chair, facing the town junta.

When Pakliotes was seated, the mayor leaned across the table toward him. Something like a smile lit up the sinister beard.

"Nice plan," the mayor said pleasantly. He twinkled his eyes at the Town Board members on either side. "Where you gonna build it?"

"What do you mean, Where'm I gonna build it? Here."

"Well, see, that's the problem. You can't."

Pakliotes bristled. "Listen here, I've built projects all over Indiana, Ohio, and Kentucky—"

"Good. Go build this one there, too," said Marvella Sweet, whose plump, malicious, smiling face was the antithesis of her name.

"You should be thanking me for wanting to build here!"

"You'll find we're an ungrateful bunch around these parts," Rex Royce drawled.

"If you're here that long," Ethel Moody, who looked to be about seven hundred years old, rasped.

"The bottom line," said the mayor, "is don't come struttin' in here with a ten-gallon hat on your half-pint head, actin' like you hung the moon, expecting us to hand you the key to Town Hall. Up in Telluride, they say you're not a local till you've spent ten winters in a row there. Well, here we say you're not a local till you got somebody with the same last name as yours buried out there in the town cemetery. Till then, you're still a damn tourist, no matter how much money you spend and how many acres you slap a No Trespassing sign on." He pushed the plans back across the table.

"Meeting adjourned."

Flammulated Owl

We were hiking down Bilk Creek on a fine autumn afternoon, after crossing Lizard Head from the pass, down those infinitely luxurious green tundra valleys twined with quicksilver waterfalls. Coming down the last leg of the trail, below the north face of Sunshine Peak, I spied something glossy and intricate scintillating in the dark moss and deadwood at the edge of the forest floor. I stopped and knelt. It was the most diminutive of owls, the size of a badminton shuttlecock.

Something was wrong with it; something stricken, crooked, to the set of the minuscule wings, the posture of the ethereal body. One eye was cockeyed and muddy. Still, it glared up at me with a look of outrage and Toshiro Mifune–like umbrage, as if it were six feet tall, not 3.6 inches.

The owl obviously couldn't fly and was completely defenseless. I decided to carry it down and then take it to a vet. Cupping the tiny thing in my hands, I ran down the trail, followed by my companions.

When we got to the trailhead, there were two cars there—two cars, but neither of them ours. We hadn't left a car at this end of the hike the way we usually do. Our vague plan had been to hitch a ride from here back up to Lizard Head, where we had left the Ford. But that plan was predicated on not being in a hurry, and now we were.

What to do? Keep going down, I decided. Eventually, we would come out in the Ilium Valley, and from there we could hike to the county jail and get a ride up to Lizard Head with one of the sheriffs. So I took off running again, my friends trailing farther and farther behind.

I was halfway down into Ilium when I heard a car approaching from above. It was a friend of ours, Julie. Her Subaru hatchback was one of the cars we had seen at the trailhead. She'd been soloing somewhere up in Bilk, come down just after we did, and now she was driving back to Telluride. She'd already picked up my three friends and heard the Owl Story. She agreed to detour up to Lizard Head Pass so we could get the Ford.

An hour later we were home, going through the phone book, trying to get hold of a vet. Unfortunately, it was Sunday. The Telluride veterinarian, her phone announced, was out of town till Sunday night, and meanwhile for emergencies please call the duck doc down in Norwood. But when we called his number, he too was out.

Meanwhile, the owl was looking none too good. We put him in a cardboard box, and he crimped himself up in a corner, unable or unwilling to stand. Too weak to glare, his gaze had turned in on itself, like he was staring into the Enormous Nothing that awaited him when his last breath failed.

"How about the Rocky Mountain Ark?" somebody suggested suddenly.

We should've called there first. Run by the doughty Lisa Margetts, on a remote hilltop on Wilson Mesa, the Ark rescued injured and sick wild animals and rehabbed them. If the animals recovered sufficiently, Lisa released them back into their original habitat; if they were too damaged to make it on their own, she let them live out their days in comfortable pens, enclosures, and cages, or just run around her house and grounds.

It was a place out of a child's dream. In one spacious chainlink enclosure, two fully grown mountain lions skulked in the brush, emerging to romp and play when Lisa or her dog Elvis came inside to visit. River otters partied perpetually in an artificial pool, waiting to be radio-collared and released on the Dolores River as part of the Colorado Department of Wildlife otter reintroduction program. A whole herd of young elk followed Lisa around wherever she went, pausing to wet-nurse off a nanny goat who provided the other half of the mothering equation. Several of these Lisa had rescued prenatally: she found the pregnant mothers dead along the highway, where they'd been hit by cars, delivered the calves by cesarean section with the aid of a vet, took them home and raised them.

In one yawning barnlike building, owls, buzzards, red-tail hawks, and bald and golden eagles roosted in the shadows. One bald eagle had been shot by some psychopath up in Alaska; his wing grew back wrong, locked up and unable to spread. When rangers found him, they figured he'd been living on the ground for close to a year, foraging and somehow dodging predators. Now he was a permanent resident of the Ark. His neighbor two perches over was a Nutty Professor hawk who liked to sit there nonchalantly as if he were thinking about something ten thousand miles away—Which came first, the hawk or the egg? or Why did the red-tail cross the sky?, and then, when the unwary visitor approached close enough, he would fire a torrent of vile excrement, big wet toothpaste squeezings of the stuff, all over his victim.

This is where we took the owl, late that afternoon, as the sun was going down behind the Wilsons. Lisa took the owl in her hands and scrutinized him. "Ha! Well, what we've got here isn't a baby, it's a fully grown flammulated owl, and this is as big as he'll get. He's like the spotted and the Mexican spotted—lives in the same old-growth forests, big trees. Looks like a predator nailed him—probably a bigger bird. His tail feathers are all chewed up, too." She looked in his eyes and tsk-tsked.

"Here, Rob, you hold him." She got a syringe with a needle fine as a horsehair. "He's got a concussion. That's bad. I'm going to shoot him up with something to bring down the swelling in his brain. If it doesn't work, I'm afraid he's not gonna make it through the night."

With incredible care, fingers steady as a stone, she slid the needle up inside his skull and pushed a tiny amber droplet from the syringe into the minuscule brain, the size of a baby's fingernail, containing all the wisdom of the ages.

We drove back down in the dusk, through meadows and groves of aspen shimmering in the wind, in the darkness.

That first night, Lisa put the owl in a cage with some newspaper to nest in and a dollop of ground-up elk meat. The next morning the owl hadn't eaten, but he'd totally shredded the paper and carefully hidden the meat beneath it. The next night he devoured all the meat, and then began to hoot, like a distress beeper: "Calling all owls—Calling all owls—" He hooted so loudly that Lisa and her husband had to move the cage outside onto the porch, and even then the persistent whooping kept them awake.

Two months later he was gone. Lisa carried him up to the forests above the Ark, less than five crow miles from where we'd picked him up. When she opened the cage, he looked at her for a moment and then sailed out the door, straight up into the ancient treetops, and was gone.

Beaver Pond

If you really love a place, you fight to save it. As mountains became Real Estate and were sold off to the highest bidder, people in Telluride changed. Not all of them, and not completely, but enough so you couldn't help but notice. Notice, and feel uncomfortable.

At the base of Bear Creek Road, there was a broad, tranquil beaver pond. It was fed by springs and runoff from Bear Creek and the ski mountain, and it drained into the San Miguel River. It had been there ever since I moved to Telluride, in '73, yet another beautiful facet of the valley. A massive beaver lodge, of dried mud, gnawed sticks, and aspen logs, rose from the water near the south bank of the pond.

Complex networks of dams, dikes, and ditches spread into the neighboring wetlands. Hiking down Bear Creek in the late afternoon you could look almost straight down into the crystal-clear heart of the Beaver Pond, see their sleek bodies rocketing along beneath the rippling skin of the water and then vanishing up into the secret world of the lodge through hidden doors. In winter, the beavers' body heat turned the lodge into a giant snow pudding that steamed cheerfully in the chilly air.

Unique hybrid cutthroat lived in the pond, swarming in caves deep under the banks. Muskrats and ducks summered there, and in the spring the willows around the shore whirred and buzzed with hummingbirds, just returned home.

And then one day in the summer of '94 it was all gone. The dam broken, the pond drained, and the beavers fled; ugly lifeless mudflats replacing vibrant living water.

It has been said that beavers built the west, and to a large degree it's true. Many if not most of our oases and fecund mountain valleys began as eroded gully-cut wastelands, where the water didn't stick around long enough to do anybody any good. Maybe a few stands of dried-up willows, just hanging on. Put a couple of beavers in there and, SHAZAM! the industrious rodents immediately start capturing the waters, reining them in. The willows thrive, responding to the raised water table and the organic goo deposited by the slowed and stilled waters. And though the beavers feed on the willows, beaver mouths contain an enzyme that acts as a growth hormone on deciduous plants, helping ensure a future crop of willows, willows forever.

In a very few years that pocket desert has become a tallgrass meadow adorned with slow, swerving streams and trout pools;

volunteer trees are moving in, and the very micro-climate has changed, become cooler, more humid. Elk graze, and migrant waterfowl stop off in their peregrinations to feed and float, cruise and snooze.

Twenty, thirty years ago, ranchers didn't hesitate to dynamite beaver lodges and dams, shoot the critters, or dead-trap them. Today, Western Slope ranchers are paying to have beavers relocated onto their lands. "It's like having two extra ranch hands," says one beef rancher with a big spread north of Grand Junction. "They ditch, they irrigate, they do flood control, they build fishing holes and grazing meadows, and I don't have to pay 'em a damn nickel. I just keep outa their way."

So what happened to the beavers in the "hip," "ecology-conscious" town of Telluride? Well, no one seems to want to talk about it now, but something like the following scenario went down.

It seems that a couple of influential home owners had built on wetlands terrain by the pond. When, almost inevitably, the beavers built more earth-and-stick works and expanded their watery realm outward, the new ponds began to threaten their houses. So what did the owners do? They called Town Hall and complained, of course. And Town Hall hired a "Beaver Expert," i.e., a howdedo hellbound hackatinny trapper, to solve the problem. He was instructed to live-trap and relocate all the Beaver Pond beavers, leaving only two, a breeding pair.

What he did was trap late in the fall, when beavers can't be relocated: they don't have enough time to dig in and gather a winter food cache in their new home. Also, several beavers mysteriously perished after being trapped (allowing the trapper to sell the pelts, of course). And the "breeding pair"? They never did reappear in the spring, if indeed they had ever existed in the first place (Pssstt! Fur hat, anybody?).

The Beaver Pond was now the Beaverless Pond.

Wild beavers still could have moved into the vacant habitat. And odds are they would have: beavers miles downstream from a newly available drainage can sense it in the water, sniff it, smell it, and they will immediately travel upstream, mile after mile, day after day, till they get to the Promised Pond.

But soon after the trapping fiasco, someone jammed a stick or two of dynamite into the base of the dam and triggered it, blowing a hole that allowed the pond's waters to drain out into the San Miguel. A fait accompli: now the beaverless Beaver Pond wasn't even a pond anymore. This was the situation a small group of us, radical hard-core Greens, found early that summer. Our first naive instinct was to call Town Hall—"Listen, there's a real emergency situation over at the Beaver Pond!" We were amazed to discover that they knew all about it. "So you must be getting ready to fix the dam, right? And then introduce some more beavers?" Only to hear that bureaucratic death knell: "Well, we're still *studying* the problem."

The last straw fell when I went walking around the ex-pond one morning and found a Rasta sitting on the old lodge, smoking a bong. It was clear what the pond's fate was going to be. It was going to remain there, an ugly mud-and-dust bowl, a place for people to poop their dogs, toss trash, and misbehave: an eyesore, a wasteland. Eventually, when everyone had forgotten there was ever a pond there, the Town Hall genii would fill in the pond bed, bulldoze it flat, and throw up some auxiliary buildings, a playground, a miniature golf course, who could tell?

Our little group—members included an old hippie realtor, a lovely soft-spoken artist from Los Angeles, a skateboard bum, and a couple of town kids on summer vacation—decided to take action. One morning, we took shovels and a wheelbarrow and headed over to the pond. We found the hole in the dam and set to work filling it. The town had a heap of neat little sandbags stashed nearby, to be used to dam off the remnant ponds left by the beavers, to placate those wetlands home owners who had gotten rid of the beavers in the first place. We decided it was only just that the bags go to patching up the dam. Soon, wheelbarrow loads of sandbags were being wheeled through the San Juan River to the dam, hoisted up onto the top, and dropped into the ragged hole left by the dynamite. As we toiled, a busybody citizen watched us and then ran off to report our activities to Town Hall.

That evening, we were informed that our work was illegal, and that if we showed up the next morning, the town marshals would come and arrest us. We consulted. Judy, our L.A. artist, was nearly in tears, but they were tears of outrage, not fear. Mike the realtor shrugged off the threat with the world-weary wisdom of someone who moonlighted as the community rabbi: "Jail, schmail." The skateboard nut and the kids thought it sounded like a great lark. And as for me, I had enjoyed the hospitality of the Colorado Penal System in the past, so there was no fear of the unknown operating there. We decided to go ahead.

Early the next morning we were shoveling dirt and rocks and tossing sandbags into the voracious hole when Telluride Marshal Norman ("No-Man," his radio deejay monicker on KOTO) Squire emerged from the bushes. He came strolling over, one hand on his service revolver.

"Quite a project you got going there," he said.

"Little help here!" The skateboarder and the rabbi were struggling to muscle a slippery boulder the size of a watermelon into the 'barrow. Norman jumped in there and lifted along with them till the rock slid over the rim safely.

"Say cheese!" When Norman looked up, Judy was snapping a photo of him abetting a misdemeanor.

Norman grinned. "Send me prints," he said. He mopped his brow and slapped ineffectually at a bug that was dancing around his glasses. "Well, you have a nice day," he said, and with that he exited the scene.

Working with redoubled energy, we attacked the hole again, and by early afternoon we had it filled. It looked tight as a drum. We cheered a few weary cheers, and then headed our various ways, triumphant.

When I came back that evening to check, I found Mike already there. He was speechless; he just looked at me, with an expression of great seriousness on his face. Then he stepped aside, and I saw what he was looking at. The pond was already half full and still rising. The springs were doing their work, pumping hundreds of gallons an hour out into the old pond bed. A few birds, swallows and such, swooped low over the pond's surface, snatching bugs out of the air.

Beaver Pond

We began to make plans for buying a pair of beavers. There was a woman up in Denver, it seemed, a six-foot-tall biker-beautician-biologist name of Sherrie Tippie, whose vocation was live-trapping beavers from threatened urban habitats, streams, ditches, and marshes in the path of "Progress," i.e., mall sites, housing developments, and highway expansions. She gave them away to ranchers, mostly on the Western Slope, veteran cattlemen who were trying to heal their damaged watersheds. All she charged was gas for her car, to haul them over from Denver.

The next afternoon I got a call from Judy, to meet her over at the pond; from her tone of voice, it sounded as if something awful had happened.

I jumped in my car and drove over. When I got there, I found Mike and Judy were staring at a dried-up pond. Mudflats, a trickle of water from the springs on the other side of the pond—and that was it.

Our first thought was that the town had struck during the night, punching the hole through the dam again. But when we looked closely, the cause was perfectly innocent: the dam had given way beneath our patching job, the current pushing against till it found the point of least resistance.

If there had been beavers in the pond, of course, they would have sensed where the dam was giving way and fixed it before disaster struck. They are capable of incredible feats of emergency engineering. A highway crew outside Denver once found a beaver dam blocking one of their culverts, and a work crew spent all day plus two hours of overtime ripping out the dam and hauling away dump truck after dump truck of sticks, boards, logs, planks, branches. When they returned the next morning, eight A.M., the dam had reappeared, constituted this time of whatever the beavers could find: a section of fence, an old bedstead from a landfill, everything but the kitchen sink and there may have been one of those in there too. They gave up, and called Tippie to come trap the beaver family and move it up into the foothills.

Of course, we didn't have any beavers; and there was no way any were going to move in till the pond was full of water and the water stayed, not in Telluride, with its myriads of dogs running loose morning, noon, and night. A full-grown beaver, with its sumoesque strength and bulldog jaws equipped with scalpel-sharp teeth, can make a dog wish it'd never been born, especially in the water, but it was too much to expect beavers to rebuild a lodge and dam on dry ground while fighting off a legion of canines.

So we played beaver once again. The inhabitants of a nearby condominium complex had been watching us work, and one of them, a genial Texan, came over with a bag of cookies and a check for $100. We ate the cookies and used the money to buy rolls of Visqueen and burlap bags, and set to work again. It took us ten hours, into the night, to build the mother of all plugs, ten hours of laboring in waist-deep mud, filling bags, putting down layer after layer of plastic, stones, and earth. We staggered home, dog-tired, callused, filthy, looking like walking relief maps. Nancy took one look at my clothes, smelled them, and then tied them up in a garbage bag and put them out on the deck, destination dumpster. There's a reason they don't make a perfume called Eau de Salamandre.

I had to go Los Angeles the next day on business, and I was gone for about a week. I flew back into Montrose, picked up my car, and drove back to Telluride. When I got to town, I headed for the Beaver Pond before I even went home.

A light drizzle was falling, speckling the surface of the water with the momentary imprint of rain. A family of ducks quacked toward me, feet paddling, looking for a handout like they had been here for years. A vee-shaped ripple cruised away to the farther shore, and a sneaky-looking muskrat emerged, looked at me over his shoulder and then slipped into the willows. Less than a yard from my feet, a school of trout swerved, catching the gray light, turning it gold. Where had they come from? How had they survived months of absolute dryness? Some subterranean pool, hidden away where the spring throbbed with last year's snow and this year's rain? There was so much we didn't know, and never would.

The next day I heard the full story. The day after I left, the dam broke again, and the pond emptied. The skateboarder, on his way to roll his way to glory on the skateboard ramp in Town Park, was the first to discover it. Enough is enough, he said to himself.

He assembled a makeshift crew, two or three of the same cynical school kids who had helped before, cynical because they are "cool" and wise beyond their years, but leap on anything genuine that comes their way with pure energy and intent. They retrieved the shovels from where we had left them in the willows along the shore and set to work.

Where we had put a dozen shovels of muck somewhere, they put 120. They dumped literally tons of rock into the gap. They retrieved the plastic sheeting and relaid it. They shoveled and shoveled and shoveled like madmen. And then they shoveled some more.

That was five days ago. The new job was holding.

We immediately got on the phone to Sherrie Tippie, and reserved the next beavers she trapped. Sherrie dealt only in beaver families, either a mated couple or a couple and their offspring. She would spend two or three extra days trapping a particularly spooky or cunning beaver rather than leave it alone while the rest of its kin got moved away. We might get two beavers, or four or five, it didn't really matter: we only hoped that they would get here in time, before the dam gave way again.

We shouldn't have worried. Less than two weeks later, I was walking around the pond early one morning when something caught my eye.

It was the bright chiselled end of a newly cut willow branch, lying in the mud, and next to it, the unmistakable webbed tracks of a *Castor canadensis*.

That night we went back out with headlamps and flashlights, and over a couple of hours we caught several glimpses of the two of them. Beavers doing what beavers do: cutting the willows along the pond's edge, cruising back toward the lodge with swatches of limbs and twigs, then returning for more. Busy as . . . yep, you got it.

I don't know how far they had come: from the old ponds in Ilium, near the batch plant, or farther, up Bilk or Big Bear, one of the San Juans' snowmelt tributaries, or way, way up beyond

Woods Lake, in the great seminal ponds in aptly named Beaver Park. But somehow, as if by ESP or magic, they had sensed this pond as soon as it was restored, from many miles away . . . waiting out our errors and failures, patiently marking time till we finally got it right . . . then and only then they had set out, heading up the drainage, toward the old ancestral lodge.

Winter's Tale

March 1981.

Who was it? I can't remember . . . Mike Grazda and one of the Farney Ranch girls and her parents. . . . They came down out of Bear Creek looking like they had seen a ghost.

It seems they had gone up on their cross-country skis to Bear Creek Boulder, the monolithic boulder at the foot of Bear Creek Falls. They took off their skis and were eating lunch next to the big rock when they heard an ominous rumble up above them, on the steep mountainside that descends into Bear Creek off the ski mountain. A monstrous dry-slab avalanche was flying down the mountain at them.

They just had time to run around to the far side of the boulder and crouch there. The slide hit, and came pouring around the boulder and over its twenty-foot top onto them. For thirty seconds or more they couldn't hear, couldn't breathe, couldn't move. "Trees were bent over; branches and small objects went by. I alternated between shutting my eyes and watching and watching the seemingly unending flood of snow," one of them recalled.

When it was finally over, they were covered with two inches of fine snow. They climbed up over the debris to the far side of the boulder where they'd left their gear. Their skis and everything else were buried under fifteen feet of snow hard as concrete. They had to walk back down, postholing through the snowpack, into Telluride. Their skis and packs didn't melt out of the snowpack till early June.

In winter, this is another world. The high country, where you wandered and gamboled all summer and fall, tries to kill you when you drop by (or climb by) for a visit. The high peaks wrap themselves in white shrouds of snow and sheaves of blue and black ice.

The avalanche chutes are locked and loaded.

Here in Telluride, we're right in the middle of it all. In 1970-something, an avalanche came all the way down over the Bear Creek Road and halfway across the Town Park softball and soccer fields, almost reaching the grandstands. And a few years ago, the tiny sky-high settlement of Ophir, just south of here, was cut off by avalanches for two weeks. To get supplies, folks had to drive down to the mouth of Ophir Valley, park their car, climb over the banks of rock-hard avalanche debris, hitchhike down to Telluride, and then hitch back again, hoping that in the meantime another slide hadn't come down and buried their car. For the last several days of the ordeal, the electricity got knocked out too. People cooked over woodstoves and propane by candlelight, and visited their neighbors on skis, headlamps lighting the way, bearing steaming fragrant bundles on their backs: casseroles, cakes, loaves of home-baked bread.

It was a dreamy, Brigadoonish spell, intensified by the fact that much of Ophir itself lies in avalanche paths, and there was the constant danger that one of those big slides might cut loose and come roaring into town, gutting two or three houses and tossing their occupants out into the freezing cold. It happens.

Back in the old mining days, avalanches were certain death for miners perched in camps and boarding houses high above timberline, on steep slopes where there was no shelter, no escape. Avalanches can generate loose snow-bearing winds of over two hundred miles an hour. People gasp for air in the tremendous pressure, opening their mouths wide to try and breathe; the airborne snow fills their lungs, chokes them, and then sets up like cement. Victims are found with snow jammed all the way out to their lips and teeth, screaming a silent, terrible terminal scream. Caught in the churning snow and slab, bodies are twisted till their heads are on backwards and their limbs contorted in impossible angles.

The miners were doomed unless they were underground, and then if rescuers didn't come, they were entombed alive. Miners still living recall the time when a whole shift of miners at Pandora was about to leave the portal at day's end, and a big loose-powder avalanche came dropping off of Ajax Mountain. The miners were driven back from the entrance by a tide of powder-like water from a high-pressure fire hose. Then the snow congealed into a solid, impenetrable wall. Take the hardest ice cube in your freezer and imagine a room full of it. Other miners from above ground had to hack and drill their way through twenty feet of this stuff to free their friends inside the Pandora.

In 1902, a series of avalanches hit the Liberty Bell Mine. The first one hit in the early morning of February 28, totally erasing the ore house, tramway station, and bunk- and boarding houses, snapping the steel tram cable and tossing the heavy ore buckets across the mountainside below. When a search party came up from town to look for survivors, another slide nearly killed them. A second search party came up the next day and was driven back by yet another avalanche. A lone miner was drinking in the Sheridan Bar when he heard about the catastrophe; he set off up toward Liberty Bell to help, and a slide took him, too. The final death toll stood at eighteen.

During the twenties, avalanches wiped out both the Black Bear and the Ajax mines, killing more miners. The snowslides almost seemed to have malign minds of their own, the Jaws or Great White Sharks of the Rockies, plucking sleeping men from a pine-plank bunkhouse and hurling them to death in the abyss below, while leaving others a few feet away untouched. Annihilating a group of miners, and then waiting, in a false calm of dim sunlight and odd drifting flakes, to pounce again on the men coming to save them.

I have never heard an avalanche joke, in all my years in the San Juans.

*　*　*

Go out in the winter mountains today, and nothing has changed. Not just back-country skiing, snowshoeing, or climbing; even a simple road trip can be a savage mix of adventure and ordeal, more drama than you ever reckoned with or wanted.

When I first moved to Telluride, my vehicle was a '64 VW camper van. It cost me $600 in Denver, and it was an excellent ride, except for the heater. The heating system on those old busses consisted of a long pipe that ran the length of the vehicle, from the engine compartment in the rear to the floorboards in front. It didn't work, not in the Rockies in winter. Only a feeble, almost imperceptible warmth wafted out onto your feet. The defrosting system was similarly screwed. I used to wear high-altitude mountaineering boots, fleece pants, arctic mitts, a balaclava, and a puffy Michelin Man parka that had once been up Everest (I bought it in Phakding from the Sherpa who summited in it for $60 and a Walkman) on my drives to Boulder, and when I arrived I inevitably tumbled out of the van onto the driveway like a fresh-frozen golem.

I kept a Kevlar Emergency Knife, purchased via an ad in *Soldier of Fortune*, beside me on the front seat to scrape the depth-hoar off the interior of the windshield. This helped make a trip across the mountains to the plains a bona fide trek . . . especially when you added in the low-tread tires, the VW's gutless performance on hills, etc., etc. A journey that should have taken eight hours or less took fourteen or fifteen, mincing along on the black-ice roller coaster of the dreadful road between Montrose and Gunnison, then the always-cold Gunnison Valley (average winter temperatures there plummeted when the damned dam builders created Blue Mesa Reservoir on the Gunnison River just west of Gunnison), and then creepy-crawling up the long grades of Monarch Pass and inch-worming down the other side on yet more ice.

Driving that road in winter, in that frigid old bus, was gloomy business indeed.

After Monarch Pass you jogged north and then east again, over Trout Creek Summit into South Park, a colossal barren basin bounded on all sides by dry, forested foothills. That took another hour and a half, ninety minutes of nothingness, and then another pass took you over into the mountain suburbs of Denver, sliding down eastward toward the city itself. Traffic was almost always terrible hereabouts, day or night, the road clogged with commuters, weekending holiday makers, and the inexplicable overflow of urban vehicles that spread beyond a city's edges.

In San Miguel County we still don't have a single stoplight, and as for stop signs, it was hard to find one that hadn't been riddled by a shotgun blast or perforated by small-arms fire. And let's face it, your typical Western Slope type didn't stop for them anyway. Just ro-o-o-olled on through, as it were, and kept on going. Here the cars and trucks traveled in convoy-like columns, due to their sheer numbers. Below, Greater Denver sprawled and smoldered in the dusk beneath a dirt-brown inversion cloud. Beyond, more strings of lights twinkled, marking the highways that stretched farther east, across the shortgrass prairies, the Great Plains, where you definitely didn't want to go, especially in winter. In that bus, you would be taken by the winds that blew unabated all the way down from the Dakotas, Montana, and Canada, winds with only a few barbed-wire fences and tall hats to slow them down, taken and flung like a Frisbee across the ice and back again, while you fought to keep yourself from crashing.

You haven't felt your feet since Fairplay. Your eyes are shot the color of rubies from staring into opaque masses of blowing snow or squinting at roads paved with ice so bright in the sun it resembles hot steel in a foundry. And after all this, where are you? Denver. Boulder. Places you left in the first place because you couldn't stand them one more day, one more minute. Kind of like leaving Lhasa to go on pilgrimage to a tire-retreading plant in Guangzhou.

The toughest winter battleground, of course, is right here in the San Juans, a few miles east of Telluride on the stretch of 550 called the Million Dollar Highway, connecting the hot spring spa resort of Ouray with the most remote town in Colorado, the tough little mining camp of Silverton. The road, following one of Otto Mears's old toll routes, is bombarded by a whole series of deadly avalanche chutes like the Mother Cline and the East Riverside, more than fifty of them total along its twenty-three-mile length.

The road's most famous tragedy took place on a Sunday morning in March of 1963. In the midst of a furious blizzard, a circuit-riding minister named Marvin Hudson came driving up from Ouray, on his way to do services for the folks in Silverton; he had his two young daughters with him. When he reached Curran Gulch, where the East Riverside slide hits the road, an auxiliary slide had just come down, blocking the way. A snow-plow operator named Leo Janes had just cleared one lane.

Reverend Hudson pulled out around the plow and tried to drive up the one lane, but his tires spun out on the loose powder on the pavement. He stopped in the middle of the road and got out to put chains on his tires. Janes was just moving to help him when the world imploded on them. A 120-mile-an-hour shock wave, bearing hundreds of tons of snow in the form of airborne powder, came slamming out of the gulch without warning. Janes's twenty-ton, forty-thousand-pound snowplow was levitated ten feet straight backward.

The road vanished into a solid mountain of snow twenty-five feet high. It took more than a week for searchers to find the remnants of the Reverend's car, crumpled like a mass of tinfoil, along with his body and that of one of his daughters. The second little girl melted out of the snowpack in May.

There are many, way too many, other tales.

In 1970, and again in 1978, the same Curran Gulch slide killed. In the 1970 incident two slides came down in quick succession, utterly destroying a snow-plowing D-7 'dozer and killing its driver, Bob Miller. And in '78, a big rotary plow with Terry Kishbaugh at the controls was clearing the aftermath of an East Riverside slide when another avalanche came down, sweeping both machine and operator away in a tidal wave of loose powder. It took a week to find what was left of the D-7; Kishbaugh's body wasn't found for another three months.

Winter gives up its dead reluctantly here in the San Juans.

The Blue Light

We're way overdue, again. Always late, here in the mountains. Trying to catch up.

Time here may be circular, infinite, but our path through it is all too linear, all too finite. Like a speeding arrow, a snowflake melting in your hand; you wish you could slow it down, but there's no way. All you can do is strive to live authentically, every moment as true as possible, nothing wasted, nothing missed.

People have taken some pretty strange paths, trying to pull that off.

Take, for instance, the two characters I will call Porcupine and Medicine Man. Back in the seventies, these two, as white as Dick Clark or Lawrence Welk, decided they wanted to be "Indi-

Fool's Gold

ans." With this in mind, they changed their names to Porcupine and Medicine Man, wore crude necklaces of roadkill feathers and beads, and bought fringed buckskin jackets. They would sit in the bars communicating with each other and anyone else who came along in guttural Pidgin—"I go Montrose tomorrow"—"We take your truck, mine no go"—interladen with nonsense syllables they thought sounded Indian. They smoked their marijuana in a red pipestone peace pipe they bought for an exorbitant sum at a trading post down in Cortez.

It wasn't an easy act to pull off, but they did it for years. Until, the stories vary, (a) they were being "Indian" in a bar down in Cortez when some genuine Navajos and Utes, unamused by their antics, beat the Indian-ness clean out of them; or (b) Medicine Man found Christ, cut off his hair, threw away his beads and feathers, and started selling Amway down in the flatlands. (Porcupine is still around but now settles for being a plain old hippie.)

Then there was Rima. She moved here in the early eighties from back east somewhere and set up housekeeping in a tepee out on Wilson Mesa, on a friend's land. She was drop-dead gorgeous: tall, with long chrome yellow hair, gleaming white teeth, clear blue eyes, and a body so fine it bordered on the ridiculous. On her, dirt, grime, and campfire smoke looked good, and cheap patchouli oil mingled with sweat and tepee funk outsmelled the Gardens of Allah. Even her hairy legs, hirsute as a coyote's, inspired the Roadhawg to rhapsodize, "I'd spend the rest of my life combing and braiding that leghair if she'd let me."

She made her living as an astrologer, and as an artist, painting clumsy Primitive oils of unicorns, satyrs, goddesses, and waifs. I

218

don't know how you tell a good astrologer from a bad one, I'm powerless in that department, but I think I know Art when I see it, and she was no Artist . . . or even artist. Her paintings were unbelievably ugly, unwieldy bodies and cartoon faces done in shrill, clashing hues of green, purple, red, black.

They sold, of course: every lecherous Telluridian with $500 to spend had a Rima, the "i" dotted with a smiley face, hanging in his home or office. (Roadhawg again: "They should throw the goddam paintings away and hang her on the wall instead.")

If I remember right, she married a rich guy from Aspen, moved there, divorced him to the tune of several mil, and ended up a highly successful Celebrity Realtor. No more tepee: the long lodgepoles still lie tumbled and forgotten in the high grass in that meadow up on Wilson.

Some made a better go of it. I always had a sneaking respect for those Telluriders who chose to squat up in the national forest in illegal shacks, shanties, treehouses, pithouses, and caves. They lived that way, they said, to spend a maximum amount of their time powder skiing, snowboarding, mountain biking, and climbing, and I believed them.

The best of the squats were truly works of love. They were carefully concealed, usually by the kind of trails the Tarahumara Indians of Mexico use to confound strangers in a land where "stranger" equals "enemy." A trail leads into the wilderness and then stops dead in the middle of nowhere. But if you walk, say, fifty feet uphill, there's the continuation of the trail, leading onward. You go along for another hundred yards, and the trail ends again. Walk downhill this time, and around back of a concealing boulder the trail begins again . . . the so-called broken trail trick.

The squats, when you finally got there, came in every variety imaginable.

One, up a creek, was a tiny one-room A-frame, like a gnome's forest house in a kid's book, nailed together tight and neat as a ship's model in a bottle. Carved wooden panels swung down to protect tiny stained-glass windows. The front door was cut from a single thick slab of redwood salvaged from some trophy-home construction project; the scrounger had carved intertwined dragons on it in deep relief. The roof, steeply peaked like a witch's hat, was cedar shingled. A steel stovepipe, wrapped at the base in fiberglass insulation, poked up four or five feet. A hatch in the roof opened to admit light and air.

The whole house couldn't have measured much more than eight feet across and stood about fifteen feet high. Inside, a Costa Rican Indian hammock hung high up in the rafters, surrounded by hanging baskets and nets containing clothes, sleeping bags, blankets, clothes, a battery-powered radio, jugs of water, juice, and granola. The floor was virtually filled by an easy chair—how did they get it up here, anyway?—and a bookcase absolutely exploding with books. Copies of *American Alpine Journal,* books on survival and travel, novels in French, guides to love-making both straight and lesbian—the woman who lived there evidently kept her options open.

Thirty feet away in the woods, a mountain bike and two pairs of skis, one cross-country, the other alpine, hung high in a tree, wrapped in plastic against the weather. To retrieve them you had to jumar up a hanging rope. Beyond that was the World's Small-est Outhouse, built along the same lines as the house.

The whole thing cost less than $500, plus sweat equity and ge-nius. I believe this was one of the Telluride squats demolished by the Forest Service a couple of years ago in a crash campaign to halt "alternative mountain living." The campaign was triggered by complaints from the good and respectable people who have moved to the Telluride area over the past decade, folks with enough money, of course, to buy their own piece of the Rockies. I am keeping the location secret in case it was one of the rare squats that survived.

Also notable was the Rasta squat in a treetop high above the north side of the valley, overlooking the mine and the graveyard. It consisted of a platform nailed and lashed to tree trunk and limbs, with a plastic geodesic dome around six feet high and twelve feet across in the center. Access was via an aluminum and nylon rope ladder, carabinered at the top to the structural four-by-fours of the platform.

The interior was a nest of carpets, bags, and blankets. Cooking went on outside, on the platform, on a twin-burner Coleman stove. Kerosene lamps and handmade candle lanterns provided light. On a winter night, with the snow falling, the dome resem-bled a fat, glowing hive, its soft light igniting the flakes into scraps of mellow gold.

The Rasta guy who built this aerie worked in town every evening as a pearl diver, skiing the days out from first tracks to sweep the mountain, commuting on mountain bike in summer and fall; on foot, x-c skis, or snowshoes when the road was snowed up. On weekends he fixed cars to supplement his income, getting work through an ad in the classifieds, hitching to job sites with his tools in his backpack. Solid life, you might say. But the Forest Service nailed his place good anyway, ripping the platform out of the tree and burning it in a gasoline-soaked bonfire.

The mountains are being made safe for people who don't really like or understand them, don't deserve them, don't belong in them.

I think the Pithouse survived, but I don't want to go up there and look, in case I'm wrong.

The Pithouse was just that, an unconscious re-creation of the Neolithic excavated in the midst of a cluster of giant boulders in a meadow high above Telluride. Too high for commuting: this was a hard-core place, for hard-core hermetic living. The builder had just moved to Telluride, freed up by a series of workmen's comp checks after a surveying accident in California. The San Juans immediately stole his heart; he was infatuated with the rocks and snow, intoxicated by the thin psychotomimetic air, enthralled by the rushing streams, the forests roaring in the wind, the silence of the stars.

After a winter and spring in a rented room in a warren of a building behind a bar on East Fat Alley, a windowless cell that smelled of hopeless human time and lives in chains, busted bathroom down the hall, he felt like he had to get into the mountains: a sensual, almost sexual desire.

When the snows melted off the high country, he packed a tent, bag, supplies, and excavating tools up into Upper Mill

Creek Basin, or maybe it was the next one over; it took several round trips, at a hundred pounds a load. He then set up camp, and started house hunting.

In less than a week, he found the spot: a jumble of contiguous boulders enclosing an area of open meadow between fifteen and twenty feet wide. A tiny melt-stream ran by less than a hundred feet away.

He started digging, pick, shovel, pry bar, and peavey. It was tough going. Four feet down he hit a boulder bigger than a beach ball; it took several days with block-and-tackle to lift it out of the hole. But by July, he had dug himself an underground dwelling with a floor six feet below the surface of the meadow. The entry-way was a steep flight of earth and stone stairs. The walls were the solid rock sides of boulders, with riprap in between. The floor was a neat tapestry of flat rocks and gravel. The roof was a custom-cut translucent plastic dome, packed up there section by section.

If he wanted to become invisible, he simply covered the plastic with turf.

The problem with many a dream house, though, is that you have to live in it, and life is not a dream. When autumn came, the Pithouse was beautiful. From his front yard he could gaze down on seas of yellow aspen and the tops of clouds grazing the treetops. He could flip back the plastic roof and sleep on his bed of boughs and thick foam pad, staring straight up at the stars, surrounded by walls of solid, living stone. Many mornings he emerged to find elk grazing out his front door; they regarded him with their deep, calm eyes and then continued to gnaw the frosty turf. They weren't used to men emerging from the earth, men who smelled like earth and seemed to be part of it. When he walked to the stream to fetch his morning tea water, the icy dew stinging his ankles, the herd parted almost imperceptibly to let him pass, then drifted back behind him.

The things he saw, that summer and fall! Mountain lions hunting. Two coyotes teaming up to hunt a whistle pig, one waiting in ambush while the other carefully pursued it in circles and parabolas till it ran right past the coyote sitting, waiting there, and—CHOMP. The great rockfall that came smashing and smiting its way down Many Marmots Peak in the middle of the night: when he heard the first rocks fall, he leapt from his pithouse in time to see the monumental rubble striking sparks the size of skyrockets off the cliffs and screes, the impact shaking the very ground on which he stood, like ten thousand bowling balls dropped down an elevator shaft. The storms that drifted around him, he was in the belly of them, a private world of hushed sounds. When you live out on the Edge or beyond it, you are privy to secrets for you and you alone.

But maybe that was part of the problem: few of us have the soul of a Captain Joshua Slocum or an Admiral Byrd and are strong enough to enjoy the earth's enormity without someone to share it.

As winter came on, and the gray snows drove through the leafless aspens, he found suddenly that he was depressed. He wasn't hungry, he wasn't curious . . . he wasn't anything. He didn't want to climb out of his sleeping bag in the morning: he just lay there, staring at the rocks around him, the light from the sky above, the fragments of spindrift whirling in under the roof. It was all Nothing to him.

Finally, one night, when the wind was howling and visibility outside was less than thirty feet, he felt a kind of revelation seize him. Laughing, he got out of his bag and started pulling on all the clothes he had. He grabbed his walking stick, picked up that Indian summer down in the aspen forests, put the headlamp on over his balaclava, climbed out of his rock hideout, and started walking. He left almost everything he owned behind and never once looked back.

He descended toward town in the storm, normally a walk of an hour and a half or two but hard going in the dark, in the storm. He skidded down through the new snow, caroming off trees, losing the trail and finding it again. Once he nearly walked right over a cliff and just caught himself in time.

It was four in the morning when he came out onto the Valley Floor by the gas station. He trudged the last mile into the darkened town so full of happiness it was all he could do to keep from whooping and jumping up and down.

When he got to town, nothing was open so he sat down on a bench and waited. Once a town marshal's car cruised by, and the cop stopped and stared at him. He waved, and the cop car moved off, vanishing in the driving snow. Welcome to the world, he said to himself. Go directly to jail, do not pass Go.

Around six A.M. Baked in Telluride opened. He went in, ignoring the stares of the workers and the other customers. With his long hair and scraggly beard and sunburnt skin, in torn windpants and a parka spangled with ice, he looked like Rip van

Rocky, but he didn't care. He ordered three onion bagels with extra cream cheese and lox, and a large coffee with infinite refills, and sat down at a table.

While he ate, he leafed through an old copy of the *Telluride Daily Planet* someone had left there. None of it made much sense, if any. There were the usual real estate ads, photos of grinning realtors offering $2.5 million log retreats in the Mountain Village, condominiums for $1.75. Time shares in the Exclusive San Miguel River Watch: the Western American Dream, buy your slice of it while you can.

He sensed people staring at him and realized he was laughing out loud. He looked around at the room, now filling up with the breakfast crowd. "Sorry," he said, but started laughing again despite himself. He stuffed his uneaten bagle in his pocket and went back out into the storm.

At nine o'clock he was outside First National Bank, waiting for the doors to open. He was the first customer of the day. He closed down his bank account, taking out all $3,272.18 in cash. Then he went to the post office and got all his back mail, six months' worth, including six disability checks in their long envelopes with the windows, the friendly green peering out at him.

He walked outside, and stood there on Main Street. Where to now? The possibilities were endless, the alternatives those of a demigod, an emperor. Still, no ideas came to him. Where to go, what to do? The snow kept falling down, and people kept looking at him, and he had no idea what to do next. He was totally lost.

In this country everything is perpetually falling, or about to fall, and gravity lurks eternally on the slippery slopes, waiting to send you ass over teakettle to Hell, or the flatlands, or the Freak Farm, or all three combined.

If you want to understand the San Juans and the people who live here, watch the 1932 German film *Das Blaue Licht,* or *The Blue Light.* Based on an actual folk legend from the Dolomite Alps in the Italian Tyrol, it is the story of a strange, haunted little town in the shadow of magical Monte Cristallo.

When the moon is full, its beams strike the summit of the peak, sending a supernatural azure light onto the town, a light with a compelling power that draws the young villagers irresistibly up onto the mountain. They climb toward the source of the light, and inevitably fall to their death. The villagers try locking their children in at night, drawing the shutters against the magnetic effulgence, but every year a few more of the young perish on Cristallo.

The only person at home on the mountain is an ephemeral young Gypsy girl named Junta. She lives in a herder's hut in the meadows at the foot of the peak, and when the full moon shines, she too is drawn up onto its cliffs and crags. Only she has the wild innocence, the voodoo: she climbs Cristallo with perfect balance and grace, like a chamois or a snow leopard. She climbs straight to the crystal-lined cave near the summit, the source of the Blue Light, where she bathes in its supernatural rays.

When she goes down to the village to sell crystals from the mountain, the peasants curse her and throw stones at her. Anyone who lives up there on the Edge, where others cannot or dare not go, is a witch, an enemy of ordinary, earthbound people.

Then one day an artist, a painter from the city, comes to the village. He seduces Junta, and stays the night with her in her hut below the mountain. When the moon rises, and Junta goes to climb the peak, he secretly follows her, all the way to the enchanted cave. The artist goes down to the village and leads the peasants, with ladders and ropes, back up Cristallo to the cave. They strip the interior of the cave of its precious crystals and haul them down to the flatlands to sell them.

The next full moon, Junta climbs Cristallo; this time, without the Blue Light to guide her, she nearly falls on her way up. When she reaches the cave, and finds it looted, destroyed, robbed of its ancient power, she falls to her death.

At the film's end we see Junta's body, miraculously intact, lying in a high meadow in the sun. Light pours from her, from the waterfalls, the forests, the streams. It is as if she has taken the Blue Light with her and preserved it forever, for timeless time.

Strangely, *Das Blaue Licht* played at the very first Telluride Film Festival, at the old Sheridan Opera House, back in 1974. There was the whole story of our mountains, right there before us on the screen. The risky Edge, and the scary sensual pull of living on it. The fear and greed of people who live in the high country but blind themselves to its beauty. The destructiveness of those who would sell it out for mere money. The exalted enduring Mystery that dwells inside those stony giants. It was all there.

And when we left the theater late that night, this is true, a full moon shone on Telluride and its mountains, Ajax, Ballard, La Junta (note that last name!), and the rest. And, ask anyone who was there, the sky was filled with a light I have never seen here before or since, except perhaps in pieces and flashes that winter night up Bear Creek with Trumbull years later: streaming off the moon, off the peaks, filling the heavens with its radiance, a hazy blue light that you couldn't turn your eyes from no matter how hard you tried.

Home Sweet
Mountain Home

I have a house at the end of a dirt road five miles west of town. My old Ford is still running, as long as you keep it in four-wheel drive. Got shelves full of books, got a pair of antique cross-country skis; got the old raft, a couple of parkas, a pair of winter boots, and a snow shovel.

It's a good life.

I'm thinking we'll drive up to Ophir this weekend and hike back over Blix Road. Built by Oskar Blix, to get up to his mine above the Upper Wasatch. His wife was the telephone operator in Telluride back then, and every summer evening she'd leave work and look up Bear Creek, to the mountainside where her husband dug for gold and silver he never found. And old Oskar, he'd come out of the tunnel, out of the depths of the mountain where he'd been working, alone except for gnomes and Tommy-knockers, and he'd signal down to her with a lantern, to tell her he was all right, and that he loved her.

They were a happy couple, those two, the old-timers say.

There are ghosts here, sure, but I'm beginning to think they're a glad-hearted bunch, after all. A laughing, singing, dancing bunch, kind of like us.

Or maybe we'll go to Columbine Lake, if it's melted off, or Rock of Ages, to find that long-lost pack.

But the thing is, of course, I don't have to go *anywhere:* I mean, I already live in the heart of the mountains, don't I? I'm already there.

My home is in the mountains: I sleep in a mountain bed, breathe mountain air, drink mountain water, and dream mountain dreams. No matter how far I roam, I carry the mountains with me, deep inside.

In this disjointed, rootless age, I've got a place. I'm the richest man in the world, even if it's only fool's gold in the end.

I guess I made it, at long last.